International Labour Organization and Global Social Governance

Tarja Halonen • Ulla Liukkunen
Editors

International Labour Organization and Global Social Governance

Springer

Editors
Tarja Halonen
Office of the President of the
Republic of Finland
Helsinki, Finland

Ulla Liukkunen
Faculty of Law
University of Helsinki
Helsinki, Finland

ISBN 978-3-030-55399-9 ISBN 978-3-030-55400-2 (eBook)
https://doi.org/10.1007/978-3-030-55400-2

This book is an open access publication.

This Springer imprint is published by the registered company Springer Nature Switzerland AG.
The registered company address is: Gewerbestrasse 11, 6330 Cham, Switzerland

Acknowledgements

The idea of this volume was born in the framework of an international seminar in September 2019 at Helsinki University to celebrate the ILO centenary. The seminar discussed the role of the ILO in the development of the social dimension of globalization from several perspectives. Our aim is to broaden the understanding of the role and relevance of the ILO today, develop new points of view and demonstrate how much we can learn from the past of this uniquely structured organization.

The preparation of this book has taken place under the exceptional circumstances of the Covid-19 pandemic and the international spread of riots. Questions of legal change, justice and fairer globalization that we took on our agenda have become an increasingly pressing challenge of our time. However, this rather highlights than undermines the essence of the mission of the ILO and makes it all the more important to continue a discourse of labour protection in the context of economic globalization.

We are grateful to the authors from three different continents for their willingness to contribute to this volume and to a number of people for their invaluable help with the preparation of the book. In particular, Le Bao Ngoc Pham, Christopher Goddard and Minna Hjort have provided assistance to this project.

Helsinki, Finland — Tarja Halonen
June 2020 — Ulla Liukkunen

Contents

Abbreviations

ADB	Asian Development Bank
AfDB	African Development Bank
AFL–CIO	American Federation of Labor–Congress of Industrial Organizations
AIIB	Asian Infrastructure Investment Bank
BSTDB	Black Sea Trade and Development Bank
CAS	Conference Committee on the Application of Standards
CEACR	Committee of Experts on the Application of Conventions and Recommendations
CFA	Committee on Freedom of Association
CJEU	Court of Justice of the European Union
CLS	Core labour standards
CSR	Corporate social responsibility
EBRD	European Bank for Reconstruction and Development
ECHR	European Convention on Human Rights
ECSR	European Committee of Social Rights
ECtHR	European Court of Human Rights
EIB	European Investment Bank
EU	European Union
EWC	European Works Council
FTA	Foreign trade agreement
GDP	Gross domestic product
GNI	Gross national income
GSP	Generalized System of Preferences
IFA	International framework agreement
IFAD	International Fund for Agricultural Development
IFC	International Finance Corporation
IFI	International financial institution
ILC	International Labour Conference
ILO	International Labour Organization
ILS	International labour standard

IMF	International Monetary Fund
IOM	International Organization for Migration
ITU	International Telegraphic Union/International Telecommunication Union
ITUC	International Trade Union Confederation
MDB	Multilateral development bank
MNE	Multinational enterprise
MNE Declaration	Tripartite declaration of principles concerning multinational enterprises and social policy
NDB	New Development Bank
NGO	Non-governmental organization
NIB	Nordic Investment Bank
NIEO	New International Economic Order
OECD	Organisation for Economic Co-operation and Development
PCIJ	Permanent Court of International Justice
SDG	Sustainable development goal
TCA	Transnational company agreement
TRIPS	Trade-Related Aspects of Intellectual Property Systems
UN	United Nations
UNCTAD	United Nations Conference on Trade and Development
UNESCO	United Nations Educational, Scientific and Cultural Organization
UNHCR	United Nations High Commissioner for Refugees
UNICEF	United Nations Children's Fund
UNPD	United Nations Development Programme
UPU	Universal Postal Union
WHO	World Health Organization
WTO	World Trade Organization

Harnessing Globalization: An Everlasting Challenge

Tarja Halonen

Contents

1 Introduction

At the turn of the century, globalization was a hot topic. Many took part in demonstrations for—or against—it. For some, globalization was a logical continuance of increasing production efficiency and of a global division of labour. Others felt that globalization only served the needs of capital and production and ignored people and their needs.

The ILO World Commission on the Social Dimension of Globalization reached a consensus to add to the UN Millennium Goals the concept of "decent work", which has been part of the Sustainable Development Goals from the start. Balanced development requires the inclusion of people and human needs.

T. Halonen (✉)
Office of the President of the Republic of Finland, Helsinki, Finland
e-mail: info@presidenthalonen.fi

T. Halonen, U. Liukkunen (eds.), *International Labour Organization and Global Social Governance*, https://doi.org/10.1007/978-3-030-55400-2_1

How did it all happen? This is how I, as someone who was involved in the process, understand and remember it. This is not an academic study or a personal memoir but rather my personal perspective on what factors and circumstances led to the emergence of a new attitude towards globalization and, moving forward, to the emergence of the idea of sustainable development. This is also a statement about the benefits and risks of globalization in the contemporary world and in these coronavirus-ridden times.[1]

2 The Historical Conflict Between Capital and Labour

2.1 The Trade Union Movement as a Proponent of Employee Benefits

The history of the trade union movement is different from country to country, but usually it has been part of or occurred in parallel with a political labour movement. Therefore, it shares the ideals of democracy, human rights and rule of law. Similarly, from early on, the trade union movement has valued international collaboration. Technological development led to the emergence of/need for industrial labour; the trade union movement arose from the need to address poor working conditions.

This was the fundamental nature of the trade union movement at the time the ILO World Commission was established, and indeed remains so to this day. When work and working environments change, new challenges are posed to employees and thereby to the trade union movement. Certain problems cannot be solved in negotiations between employer and employee, but require broader, structural solutions. This calls for extensive collaboration across different areas of society.

The World Commission also adopted this broad-based approach. Its proposals extend beyond the original focus of work-related issues. This was deliberate. Juan Somavia, then Director-General of the ILO, was closely connected to the World Commission, and shared our thinking,[2] through the founding letter of the World Commission as well as through the selection of its members.

My co-chair, Benjamin William Mkapa, and I strove to paint an optimistic picture of opportunities for change, even though we did not have a mandate or even a desire to present a proposal outside the ILO. However, I knew, of course, that the issue had been broadly discussed within the UN family. The hopes and desires for change turned out to be tremendous. This is how we, the co-chairs of the ILO World Commission, phrased it: "Our proposals are ambitious but feasible. We are certain that a better world is possible."[3]

---

[1] This article is a translation from Finnish into English.

[2] ILO (1999).

[3] World Commission on the Social Dimension of Globalization (2004), p. ix.

2.2 Controversial Tripartism

It is probably worthwhile to underline that this awakening came early, compared to many other national developments in the history of political and professional labour movements.

When the ILO was established in 1919, the rights of workers and their structurally weaker contractual status were on the table. Trade unions were the natural answer. However, it was also clear that improving the status of employees is only possible in a democratic state that recognises the equal rights of all individuals. Rule of law and good governance also protect the status of workers. A state has a general obligation to protect its people, and therefore all employees.

Recently, the triangle—employers, employees, the government—as contractual parties has gained less attention. However, in exceptional times, employers also seem to be more willing to adopt a more positive approach to the tripartite system. The trade union movement is needed to bring a nation together. Tripartism was also a central philosophy in the rebuilding of Europe after the Second World War and during the financial crises early in the millennium. Currently, we are seeing signs of this during the coronavirus epidemic of 2020.

Throughout the decades, the ILO has shown interest in tripartism to a varying degree. It gained increasing importance in the 1960s and came back into focus at the turn of the millennium. Strong nation states are also needed to keep globalization in check.

3 Global Responsibility and Solidarity

The World Commission was not operating alone or in a void. For many, the Millennium Development Goals, set by the UN in 2000, represented the first statement in favour of global social justice.[4] The Goals are not a legally binding commitment but, rather, a political commitment. The member states took them quite seriously, though. Developing countries in particular considered them a major win. They could have been implemented more quickly but the UN monitored them closely and addressed some of their shortcomings.

I followed this process closely, because the Millennium Summit of September 2000 was jointly presided over by Finland and the exiting Presidency of the UN General Assembly, Namibia. My country was about to take over. It is customary in the UN that important summits are co-chaired by representatives of North and South, as was the case in 2000.

I had been elected President of Finland in our March elections, and therefore co-chaired the historic meeting with President Sam Nujoma of Namibia. Former Prime

[4] Resolution adopted by the UN General Assembly: United Nations Millennium Declaration (A/RES/55/2).

Minister Harri Holkeri assumed the role of President of the United Nations General Assembly during Finland's one-year presidency. I knew him well. When I was a minister for the first time, it was in the Holkeri government of the 1980s. Looking back, the Millennium Development Goals were a great achievement. Poverty—extreme poverty in particular—declined. Disparities of wealth continued to grow, however.

Progress was made in healthcare: the number of women and children dying during childbirth shrank significantly, and the infant mortality rate declined dramatically. Girls' and women's health still lagged behind that of men and boys. Many more girls and boys gained access to primary education, but the quality of education failed to meet expectations. Girls' education was too often interrupted by family obligations.

Plans were made to address social injustice through development cooperation. In the Monterrey Consensus, the countries involved endorsed giving at least 0.7% of their GNI in official development assistance, in which education and healthcare would play a central role in tackling extreme poverty and hunger. Many felt an urgency to remove injustice from the prevailing economic system. The role of women needed to be improved.[5]

The key message of the Millennium Development Goals was global solidarity; yet, they did not mention the world's most common source of income: work. There was also no reference to social security. From this point of view, too, the Report of the World Commission on the Social Dimension of Globalization was a welcome addition.

4 Globalization: A Multifaceted Challenge and an Opportunity

4.1 Globalization Changed the Way We Work

The emergence of an international division of labour was a lengthy process. At the turn of the millennium, different parts of the world witnessed it differently. Generally speaking, there was a division between industrial countries and developing countries—between North and South. A closer look showed that there were winners and losers in both groups. There were also winners and losers within individual countries.

In Europe and North America, globalization was largely considered to involve a division of labour related to increasing production efficiency. The invention and use of new technology after the Second World War strengthened opportunities—and the need—for an international division of labour. In a way, information technology shrank the world. But what makes production more efficient does not necessarily benefit the worker.

[5] UN (2003).

Globalization did, however, give poor countries a new opportunity to narrow down the income gap and not just to the traditionally poorer countries of the global South but also to industrial countries with a smaller economy—such as my own country, Finland. We remained a well-educated and agile country that was able to create such phenomena as Nokia. It can be said that Finland's Linus Torvalds created an operating system that now runs a large part of the internet. Globalization appears to provide unprecedented opportunities for economic growth, not to mention improved health and wellbeing.

In Africa, Asia and Latin America, globalization is typically considered part of the same continuum as colonialism. The opinions of the members of the World Commission reflected these diverse views. The Millennium Development Goals were seen as the beginning of global compensation programmes. The Monterrey Financing for Development conference, whose goal was to increase official development assistance from 0.7% of GNI, had boosted faith in the changes under way. The Asian members of the World Commission were more optimistic than other developing countries about being able to close the divide between them and European countries and the USA by means of globalization. Upon closer inspection, we see that most new investments were made in the two largest Asian countries: China and India.

What the workers and labour representatives of different countries had in common was a concern that people and their needs would be sidelined by globalization. Demonstrations against globalization grew larger. People opposed the exportation of jobs to developing countries. Multinational enterprises in particular were seen as the culprits. At the same time, governments were blamed for not protecting their citizens against unemployment. The international finance world was blamed for supporting large corporations.

In a market economy, governments had limited possibilities to protect jobs, however. They mostly encouraged companies to retrain former employees who had been left jobless because of globalization. However, the training and reassignment of unemployed people was insufficient. Those with less education lost jobs, and any new jobs were given to younger people with a higher education. In the "old" industrial countries, too, society became polarised into proponents of and opponents to globalization.

Let's take a practical example:

> In February 1997, the French car manufacturer Renault decided to close its plant in Vilvoorde, Belgium. After making the decision to cease manufacturing, Renault announced it publicly without first informing or consulting its European Works Council. The announcement was followed by demonstrations and a strike that took place simultaneously in Belgium, France and Spain, of which the latter was to be the new home of the former Vilvoorde operations. The case was brought to court in both Belgium and France. This did not stop Renault from closing down its Vilvoorde plant, and most of the employees lost their jobs.[6]

[6] For a discussion of the many legal dimensions and legal procedures related to the case, see Liukkunen (2005), p. 20.

The European Union, alongside many other international organisations and governments, still had faith in managed globalization.

Thus, in a way, the tripartite principle behind establishment of the World Commission on the Social Dimension of Globalization was a natural consequence in addressing the polarising political situation at the time.

4.2 Multinational Corporations: Aspirations of Autonomy

Multinational corporations grew rapidly. Their size was a challenge not just for the trade union movement but also for governments. They adopted a discourse according to which multinational corporations had no home base. They seemed to want to form an independent community of their own, outside the jurisdiction of any country. The role of nation states as defenders of their people became weaker.

At the same time, large corporations in particular started to streamline operations by outsourcing non-core functions, such as cleaning and transportation, to formally independent operators. In reality, these subcontractors did not become independent entrepreneurs but subcontractors who were completely dependent on the head company. Their status was similar to that of employees, but health and safety rules and social security did not apply to them.

Furthermore, particularly in developing countries, many workers were excluded from employment calculations. Many agricultural workers belonged to this group. They did not own the land they were cultivating, yet they were not counted among the employees of the landowner. Most of these workers came from developing countries but, because of their status, they were not eligible to take part in any of the training or support programmes provided in the development cooperation agreement. Thus, these people were not covered by employee health and safety or job security schemes, nor were they eligible to receive entrepreneur benefits.

In many developing countries, the share of such informal work was, and still is, significant. There are many reasons for this phenomenon: the remnants of colonialism, the legal underdevelopment of ownership, women's limited rights to own land, and so forth. Informal work was keeping people alive but at great risk.

These are the reasons why we in the World Commission considered it absolutely necessary to address both the issues and the solutions much more broadly than labour legislation would have permitted. We considered it a political rather than a legal question.

4.3 A Polarised World

The world had become polarised in many ways. The UN Millennium Development Goals set at the turn of the millennium remain founded on global solidarity and justice. They can also be seen as an attempt to mitigate the divide created by globalization between the wealthy global North and the poor South. They did not, however, highlight the fact that poverty could also be found in the industrial North. Unemployment was rising, and the standard of living was declining in many previously wealthy areas. People lost faith in the future. While awareness of the help needed in the poor global South was increasing, unemployed industrial workers did not consider themselves oppressors of the South. A breeding ground for political extremism and populism was created.

The international sentiment was already getting bleaker. On 11 September 2001, Al Qaida destroyed the twin towers of the World Trade Center. Hundreds of people died in a matter of minutes. The USA declared war on terrorism. Fear and deep mistrust spread across the world. It seemed unlikely that any new international treaties could be concluded.

The Millennium Development Goals were a diplomatic surprise of sorts. They raised important issues ranging from poverty to health and education. They did not, however, mention work as a source of wellbeing. The Millennium Declaration was agreed upon at the UN relatively quickly but resources for its implementation were lacking. Concrete follow-up was also needed.

4.4 The World Commission Was Also Welcomed by the UN Family

In this polarised situation, the ILO decided to establish a World Commission to investigate the social dimension of globalization.[7] It was a rather bold attempt to bring a highly split group—all with good arguments—to the same table. The World Commission, set up in 2002, was welcomed into the UN family: not to the UN itself but to the ILO, its agency organisation in Geneva.

The chairs and members of the World Commission formed a diverse group from around the world. The aim was to guarantee that the World Commission would have broad-based expertise on the many aspects of globalization. The members represented employers, trade unions, governments, academia and civil society, including the women's rights and indigenous peoples' movements.

Its diversity was both a blessing and a challenge. We spent a significant share of the relatively limited time we were given in building trust between different parties. This so-called honeymoon period was relatively successful. In my opinion, everyone was interested in each other's perspectives. Where else could the CEO of a large Japanese corporation have had reason or the time to learn about the experiences of a South African freedom fighter, or a European statesman ask a nurse working with the indigenous peoples of the Philippines for their opinion on how globalization was affecting people's living conditions?

[7] ILO (2004a).

More attention was paid to differences between the lives of women and men, but it remained a minor theme in the talks, despite the participation of many active women and informed men. The strong and vivid presentations given by Ruth Cardoso and Hernando de Soto from Latin America have stuck in my mind. Gender equality issues were being raised across the world, but this was less obvious in the World Commission than in some other UN events. In the final version of the text of the Commission report, however, equality featured quite strongly.

We were lucky to have an excellent secretariat that had already worked on defining our scope within the ILO. The members of the World Commission included economic policy experts such as Joseph Stiglitz and Hernando de Soto, who, together with Giuliano Amato, the former prime minister of Italy, and German politician Ernst Ulrich von Weizsäcker, joined forces to take an in-depth look at the relationship between economic development and democracy.

China was represented by Lu Mai who comes from a research institute and was a very active participant. We also visited China. The World Commission marked the beginning of long-term collaboration between myself and several other members, including Valentina Matvienko from Russia, who was then the Mayor of St. Petersburg. The members of the World Commission were not only top experts but also charming personalities.

I had not met my co-chair, Benjamin William Mkapa from Tanzania, before. After spending hours with him and the Secretariat planning future action and discussing what might be realistic steps to take, we became close. Some of the members of the World Commission were well-known and had long careers, while for others, their careers were just about to take off. All in all, I would like to say that cooperation between the members of the World Commission left me with an excellent impression of competence and cooperation, which I benefited from on many later occasions. The ILO's Director-General, Juan Somavia, had built a solid foundation.

Once, at a World Commission summit, I attempted to sum up the different viewpoints of the participants. I likened globalization to a train that runs on its own tracks, fuelled by its own power. Industrial countries were seated in first class, having purchased tickets with other people's money. Asians were sitting on hard seats in third class. And Africans were still waiting at the station, wondering whether they should get on the train or not. Victoria Tauli-Corpuz, who represented the indigenous peoples of the Philippines, said it seemed to her that the train was running on their land without permission, while they just kept trying to avoid getting run over by it.

5 Proposals of the World Commission

The practical near-future objective of the World Commission was to add decent work and employment to the ILO principles, the UN Millennium Development Goals and, possibly, the goals of other international organisations. The same aim was also to be included in government programmes.

The World Commission's suggestions for fair globalization involved several levels. The most comprehensive aim was to change the fundamental nature of globalization: to move away from narrow, production-centric thinking towards a broad-based approach attentive to the needs of the people. In addition to the economy, democracy, human rights and good governance must be promoted.

Corporations and other economic actors must abide by these rules just like everyone else. The most radical idea of the World Commission was to incorporate employment and the democratisation of labour into a more socially just world. We were of the opinion that globalization had taken a wrong turn because it materialised people. People want to earn a living and social independence through working: doing something that others consider to have exchange value. Thus, work is important not only because it provides a livelihood but because it integrates people in society. To put it conversely, working life is part of a democratic society where all the same laws apply as elsewhere in society.

Respect for human rights in working life was an integral element of ILO core labour standards.[8] This means that forced and child labour are banned. All people must have the same human rights, including freedom of expression and freedom of association. Workers must have the same human rights inside and outside their workplaces. Thus, an employer's power over an employee is not unlimited. The World Commission viewed core labour standards and respect therefor as important. Moreover, social dialogue is needed. The right to organise and collective bargaining are core elements of social dialogue.

I have sometimes been asked why we chose the phrase "decent work". We did not want to use the word "good" because of its connotations. The terms "good job" and "good life" did not convey what we wanted. Decent means that we are not quite there yet but very close; and "decent" is also a synonym for "fair". It was a realistic objective that we could build on. It is a global demand. It must be true everywhere. I remember the ILO Secretary-General, Juan Somavia, thinking along the same lines even before that. However, I was not involved in the process at that point.

The work of the World Commission was marked by an optimistic view of people's ability to control the world and globalization. We believed that globalization

---

[8] See ILO, Declaration on Fundamental Principles and Rights at Work. Adopted by the International Labour Conference, 86th Session, Geneva, 18 June 1998 (Annex revised 15 June 2010). The Declaration underlines four core labour standards, namely freedom of association and the effective recognition of the right to collective bargaining, the elimination of all forms of forced or compulsory labour, the effective abolition of child labour, and the elimination of discrimination in respect of employment and occupation.

would increase the efficiency of production, benefit individuals and societies alike and integrate humanity in a way that would make conflicts and wars less likely.

6 Globalization Management Starts with a Strong State and Continues with International Collaboration

Many globalization scholars have theorised that nation states would become less important as globalization gains strength. This would probably be the case if the market economy had developed freely under globalization. Such a development would probably not attend to human needs and desires.

The World Commission had faith in the nation state because, at the moment, the state is the largest unit that people can impact. Therefore—without underestimating international organisations—we should try to make states stronger, instead of wishing them to grow weaker. They still constitute the best protection for the people. However, citizens should be more aware of what their representatives do in international forums.

In addition to globalization itself, the World Commission wanted to draw strong focus on attempts by financial market operators to impact the way countries can control the detrimental effects of globalization. For example, developing countries were pressured to allow movement of investments and capital as freely as possible, even though it was known that the rapid liberalisation of finance had proved highly destabilising to economic policymaking in a number of nations from Latin America to East Asia. The report of the World Commission states that developing countries should be allowed to take a cautious approach to freeing up movements of capital.[9] World trade rules hindered this type of selective protection or strategic promotion of domestic industries that played a part in the economic development of successful industrialised countries in Europe, North America and Asia. Some of these proposals were adopted.

Thus, international organisations should democratise their own rules and improve the efficiency of their own operations and mutual cooperation. The UN reform has been ongoing during the term of every UN Secretary-General of this millennium. It takes a long time. There should also be closer cooperation between the specialised agencies of the UN. According to the World Commission, special attention must be paid to coordination or collaboration between the UN and organisations close to it, such as Bretton Woods institutions.[10]

The international community continued to have the same kind of optimism as when the Millennium Development Goals were set. They believed that comprehensive management of global economic policy could be achieved, even though negative phenomena such as the accumulation of wealth, polarisation and the crisis of

---

[9] World Commission on the Social Dimension of Globalization (2004), pp. 90 and 114.

[10] Ibid., pp. 113–114.

financial capitalism were present. The World Commission's idea of a comprehensive and multipolar but controllable globalization lives on.

The Millennium Development Goals made few references to the environment. The report of the World Commission did not highlight environmental impacts in any major way. It was not until the Sustainable Development Goals—the Rio Summit[11] and Agenda 2030[12]—that nature and the environment, gender equality and the status of women were brought to the fore.

7 Did the World Commission's Objectives Change the World?

The report of the World Commission sparked discussion around the world.[13] Even during the working stage, the Commission made its work visible not only through its diverse membership but also through its meetings and visits around the world. This was effective, albeit arduous.

The ILO approved the recommendations of the report, which was submitted to its Governing Body and the International Labour Conference (ILC) in 2004.[14] Also the Director-General of the ILO submitted his proposals to the ILC for a strategic response to the World Commission's recommendations, covering some of the key fields of work of the ILO: national policies to address globalization, decent work in the global production system, growth, investment and employment, a socio-economic floor, international migration, the international labour standard system, and the role of tripartism.[15]

Today, fair globalisation is one of the mainstream strategies of the ILO addressed in its programmes across the world.[16]

Decent work was added to the Millenium Development Goals in 2005.[17] It has been part of the Sustainable Development Goals from the start.

---

[11] See Resolution adopted by the UN General Assembly on 27 July 2012: The future we want (A/RES/66/288).

[12] See Resolution adopted by the UN General Assembly on 25 September 2015: Transforming our world: the 2030 Agenda for Sustainable Development (A/RES/70/1).

[13] ILO (n.d.-a), ILO (2004b); Resolution adopted by the General Assembly on 2 December 2004: A fair globalization: creating opportunities for all – report of the World Commission on the Social Dimension of Globalization (A/RES/59/57).

[14] ILO (2004c).

[15] ILO (2004d).

[16] See, for example, ILO (n.d.-b, n.d.-c). See also ILO Declaration on Social Justice for a Fair Globalization. Adopted by the International Labour Conference, 97th Session, Geneva, 10 June 2008.

[17] Resolution adopted by the UN General Assembly on 16 September 2005: 2005 World Summit outcome (A/RES/60/1), para 47.

Decent work has featured widely in different UN programmes.[18] I have myself twice been part of UNCTAD reform processes. In addition, the IMF has, to some extent, included the recommendations of the World Commission in its policies.[19]

8 Epilogue or: What's Next, Globalization?

Globalization evolved into an effort to increase production efficiency. It was the next step of internationalization and the international division of labour. Without a doubt, globalization has in many ways been a great economic success; it has also played a part in tackling poverty. During the course of its evolution, globalization has become more cost efficient but also increasingly vulnerable. Furthermore, it has not proven to be as independent or omnipotent as its most fervent fans have led us to believe, because even a multinational corporation operates on national territory or territories. Nation states tend not be controlled by individual companies, even though the financial—and thereby political—influence of multinational corporations has greatly increased. It takes time to worm one's way into a societal power structure. To assume political power, multinational companies can use semi-democratic means and pressure decision-makers to give them tax benefits by arguing that these would boost employment or otherwise benefit voters. We have learned from court cases around the world that heads of state, government leaders and officials sometimes take bribes.

The free movement of goods and services is a prerequisite for free trade. Multinational companies would not be able to operate without bilateral or multilateral cooperation between governments. In most nation states, citizens have some influence over the choice of the country's decision-makers. This requires that they believe that they can benefit from the issues that their elected leader or leaders are lobbying for. This should also be the case with free trade and globalization.

Globalization will not disappear, and nor will nation states. Therefore, their mutual relationship must be rebuilt in a more sustainable way. A more humane but also economically more efficient form of globalization is only possible with the support of strong and democratic nation states that are open to international collaboration.

People desire financial wellbeing and social justice; that is the kind of development they are looking for. At the same time as the ILO World Commission was working on its report, the UN Millennium Development Goals were already being implemented. The action programme, which emphasised social justice, was launched in 2004. In 2015, the Sustainable Development Goals were approved and they contain the same principles as the programme, with an added demand for

[18] See, for example, UN Women (n.d.) and UNDP (n.d.).

[19] Jenkins et al. (2007), paras 89 and 97.

environmental welfare.[20] The link between these factors is logical and straightforward but, with so many of them to address, implementing changes is increasingly difficult. Furthermore, employment has been awarded relatively little attention in the programme-setting for sustainable development even though unemployment or fears of unemployment are among the key reasons behind the rise of populism.

The report of the ILO World Commission on the Social Dimension of Globalization covers a lot more than just decent work and employment. Globalization as a philosophy is in need of comprehensive reform. Sustainable development is founded on human rights, democracy and rule of law: they build trust between people. This trust must extend to globalization. The World Bank in particular along with the IMF appears to have come to realise the significance of rule-based international collaboration. As early as the financial crisis of 2008, governments were forced to pause and consider the warning given by the World Commission regarding the risks of unregulated international finance capital.

The problems that the European Union has faced with the single European currency have starkly demonstrated the significance of collaboration and honesty—or rather the consequences of a lack thereof. Member States have committed to a single currency but hesitate to observe a common monetary and financial policy without legally binding rules. This is one of the topics addressed by the Nobel-prize winning Joseph Stiglitz in this volume.[21]

The direction in which the WTO has developed in the 2000s is a stark reminder of the fundamental problem related to globalization, or rather the market economy. Even if capital and production dictated these rules, any mutually-agreed rules aiming to promote change would be overrun by a struggle for the survival of the fittest. The World Trade Organization getting stuck in court is a great example:

> The crisis of the WTO's dispute settlement system began on 10 December 2019, when the term of two of the remaining three Appellate Body members expired. As the United States refused to initiate the selection process and appoint new members to the organization's Appellate Body, the Members were unable to reach a consensus to fill the vacant positions.[22] With only one member in office, the Appellate Body has become dysfunctional and is unable to hear new appeals. The blockade of the Appellate Body has paralyzed the two-tiered dispute settlement system in the WTO. Despite the members' attempts to restore a fully functioning Appellate Body, the impasse remained unresolved.[23]

---

[20] Resolution adopted by the UN General Assembly on 25 September 2015: Transforming our world: the 2030 Agenda for Sustainable Development (A/RES/70/1).

[21] See Stiglitz (2020).

[22] See WTO (2020) Minutes of Meeting of the General Council, Geneva, 9–10 December 2019, pp. 12–33.

[23] See WTO (2020) Minutes of Meeting of the Dispute Settlement Body, Geneva, 27 January 2020, pp. 14–19.

8.1 The Future of Labour

The world and, with it, the world of labour have changed rapidly since the report of the ILO World Commission on the Social Dimension of Globalization was published. The report of the ILO Global Commission on the Future of Work, titled "Work for a brighter future", is a statement on this topic. It does not deny the future existence of globalization but requires that social justice be observed in its implementation.

Furthermore, people want to feel useful. Therefore, demands for livelihood or, for example, a universal basic income—which has gained popularity in the Nordic countries in particular—were not the only focus; rather, the significance of people was. Work is gaining increasing importance. For example, youth surveys from Finland point to a similar trend, showing that young people want to do work that matters and that they are not merely motivated by the opportunity to earn money.

In order to make this dream a reality, the ILO Global Commission on the Future of Work suggests that we invest in people not only through education but also through work and work-related institutions. In other words, labour must have an economic, humane and environmental impact. Future society will be increasingly information-based, and this requires the creation of opportunities for life-long learning.

8.2 What Can We Learn from the Coronavirus (COVID-19) Epidemic?

As I am writing this in April 2020, we do not yet know what returning to so-called "normal" will look like once the epidemic is over. However, we already know that this epidemic has had an unexpectedly significant impact on people's health and wellbeing.

Tackling the coronavirus has required both a national and an international effort. Currently, the infection rate is approximately 3.1 million, and the death toll is roughly 223 thousand.[24] The virus does not recognise national or other borders. For comparison, a total of 2.7 million people die from work-related reasons each year.

This tiny little virus turned our world upside down in what seemed like seconds: it emptied our calendars, closed our borders and made us change our behaviour both voluntarily and by coercion.

In addition to human suffering, the corona epidemic sparked a dire economic downturn. We are yet to learn its scope. The virus also forced people to consider the production-related, economic and humane consequences of globalization.

We realised how dependent we are on each other. We missed our families and friends in different ways—but we also missed being able to simply "be" safely

[24] WHO (2020).

around other people at school, at work, and in cafes, shops and parks. In other words, being human amongst other humans.

If there is a lesson to learn from COVID19 it is that our world is highly fragile.

The ways in which globalization developed, or was developed, resulted in a gigantic but extremely vulnerable system. An increasing number of people have come to observe how fragile the foundation of globalization is: a system driven by profit-making alone is simply not compatible with sustainable development. Economic production systems must be able to operate under common rules, not outside them.

I am an optimist. I believe that we want to change the world and that we will indeed change the world.

References

ILO (1999) Report of the Director-General: Decent work, International Labour Conference, 87th Session, Geneva, 1999. International Labour Office, Geneva

ILO (2004a) World Commission on the Social Dimension of Globalization. Available at: https://www.ilo.org/fairglobalization/origins/lang%2D%2Den/index.htm. Accessed 30 Apr 2020

ILO (2004b) Reply by the Director-General to the discussion of his report, International Labour Conference, 92nd Session, Geneva, 2004. International Labour Office, Geneva

ILO (2004c) ILO Governing Body welcomes report of World Commission on the Social Dimension of Globalization. Available at: https://www.ilo.org/global/about-the-ilo/newsroom/news/WCMS_005189/lang%2D%2Den/index.htm. Accessed 30 Apr 2020

ILO (2004d) A fair globalization. The role of the ILO. Report of the Director-General on the World Commission on the Social Dimension of Globalization, International Labour Conference, 92nd Session, Geneva, 2004. International Labour Office, Geneva

ILO (n.d.-a) References to the report of the World Commission on the Social Dimension of Globalization. Available at: https://www.ilo.org/legacy/english/fairglobalization/download/reference.pdf. Accessed 30 Apr 2020

ILO (n.d.-b) Decent Work Country Programmes (DWCPs). Available at: https://www.ilo.org/global/about-the-ilo/how-the-ilo-works/departments-and-offices/program/dwcp/lang%2D%2Den/index.htm. Accessed 30 Apr 2020

ILO (n.d.-c) International Programme on the Elimination of Child Labour (IPEC). Available at: https://www.ilo.org/ipec/lang%2D%2Den/index.htm. Accessed 30 Apr 2020

Jenkins H, Lee E, Rodgers G (2007) The quest for a fair globalization three years on: assessing the impact of the World Commission on the Social Dimension of Globalization. International Labour Organization (International Institute for Labour Studies), Geneva

Liukkunen U (2005) Globalisaatio, EU ja henkilöstön osallistuminen [Globalisation, the EU and employee participation]. Edita, Helsinki

Stiglitz J (2020) Postscript. In: Halonen T, Liukkunen U (eds) International Labour Organization and global social governance. Springer, Cham

UN (2003) Monterrey consensus of the international conference on financing for development. United Nations Department of Public Information, New York

UN Women (n.d.) SDG 8: promote sustained, inclusive and sustainable economic growth, full and productive employment and decent work for all. Available at: https://www.unwomen.org/en/news/in-focus/women-and-the-sdgs/sdg-8-decent-work-economic-growth#:~:text=UN%20Women%20acts%20to%20achieve,distribution%20of%20unpaid%20care%20work. Accessed 30 Apr 2020

UNDP (n.d.) Goal 8: decent work and economic growth. Available at: https://www.undp.org/content/undp/en/home/sustainable-development-goals/goal-8-decent-work-and-economic-growth.html. Accessed 30 Apr 2020
WHO (2020) Coronavirus Disease (COVID-19) Dashboard. Available at: https://covid19.who.int/. Accessed 30 Apr 2020
World Commission on the Social Dimension of Globalization (2004) A fair globalization: creating opportunities for all. International Labour Office, Geneva. Available at: https://www.ilo.org/public/english/wcsdg/docs/report.pdf. Accessed 30 Apr 2020

President Tarja Halonen was the 11th President of the Republic of Finland (2000–2012) and Finland's first female head of state. President Halonen is famous for her special ties with the core activities of the ILO. During 2002–2004, she co-chaired the ILO World Commission of the Social Dimension of Globalization. From March 2009 until September 2014, she served as the Chair of the Council of Women World Leaders. In August 2010, President Tarja Halonen was appointed co-chair of the UN Secretary-General's High-level Panel on Global Sustainability. She was the co-chair of the High-Level Task Force for ICPD from 2012 to 2016. From 2015 to 2017, President Halonen served as a member of the World Bank World Development Report 2017 Advisory Group. She continues to promote issues related to sustainable development in her many other roles, including, as a member of Sustainable Development Solutions Network's Leadership Council, as a member of Pan-European Commission on Health and Sustainable Development and as a Chair of Lancet-SIGHT commission on Peaceful Societies through Health and Gender Equality. In Finland, she serves as the Chair of the Board of the University of Helsinki, is a member of the Board of SITRA and is also chairing the Board of the Finnish National Gallery.

The ILO and Transformation of Labour Law

Ulla Liukkunen

Contents

1 Introduction

In a globalizing world, questions of working life remain central to most people.[1] These questions place at the centre individuals and their well-being, and they offer perspectives of vulnerabilities to society that voices of the globalization of economy tend to sideline. But while norm-setting for international economic relations has been considered central to global governance, norm-setting for the governance of the social dimension of globalization has been greeted with less enthusiasm. Recently, we have been witnessing times where the economic transformation has led to accumulating challenges to labour protection that have turned out increasingly difficult to overcome. The objectives of the oldest UN agency, the ILO,

[1] As the ILO Commission of the Social Dimension of Globalization stated in its report, globalization affects people most directly through their work. See World Commission on the Social Dimension of Globalization (2004), p 64.

U. Liukkunen (✉)
Faculty of Law, University of Helsinki, Helsinki, Finland
e-mail: ulla.liukkunen@helsinki.fi

T. Halonen, U. Liukkunen (eds.), *International Labour Organization and Global Social Governance*, https://doi.org/10.1007/978-3-030-55400-2_2

have met obstacles that seem to flow directly from the way economic-political globalization has been writing the regulatory agenda for states.[2]

The effects on the labour market of globalization of the world economy have been altering the role of traditional regulatory actors. In recent decades, states and social partners, the actors that work tripartitely in the ILO towards social justice and international labour standards, have confronted changes in their position that have made them weaker builders of a better working life. States' ability as regulatory actors has diminished as increasingly often they face situations beyond the reach of their legislative powers. For the social partners, declining coverage of collective agreements has meant changes in their position and regulatory power. Consequently, the role of labour law has also been changing. With a strong emphasis on economic competition, the post-industrial era has come to mark a profound change in conceptions of the objectives and functions to be set for labour law.

States have started to respond to global economic competition with regulatory strategies that tend to highlight flexibility over labour protection. This trend has gained support from international financial institutions that have long argued for flexibility and deregulation of the labour market.[3] It has been suggested that labour law models need an adjusted framework to enable more competitive flexibility. Simultaneously there are demands for more inclusive regulatory approaches as old categorizations in labour law are building divides that strongly impair working individuals.[4] The idea of employment contract-centred labour law has come under mounting question.[5] Increasingly, not only the regulatory model of labour law but also its foundations, in terms of substance, sphere and institutions, have been put to the test with new labour market realities.

Against this background, the ILO as an organization appears to have been given an almost impossible task to promote social justice and fairer globalization.[6] A weaker commitment to workers' human rights seems to be a direct consequence of a global legal environment where the power of states as regulatory actors is not the same as hitherto. As the ILO's governance model is based on tripartism, efforts on the part of the organization have become more challenging also with the development of the diminishing power of the social partners. We are witnessing both institutional and regulatory changes to the labour market that push forward decentralization of collective bargaining. The entire industrial relations infrastructure has been changing so that legal-institutional structures have been affected. Meanwhile, the transnational dimension of labour law has been evolving, providing a new normative basis for transnational industrial relations and cross-border collective contractual arrangements.

---

[2] For a critical account of the imbalance from a labour law perspective, see Maupain (2013).

[3] See, for example, Weiss (2013), p. 7.

[4] Critically, see Langille (2019a).

[5] See Davidov (2002).

[6] See Maupain (2013).

This article discusses some of the biggest challenges to the ILO caused by the altering scene of globalization and collective labour law regulation. It examines the recent transformation of collective bargaining regimes at national and transnational level and the consequences for normativities that characterize the relationship between labour law and the system of international labour standards. The transformation of labour law highlights developments that deserve attention when we consider the role of the ILO at the beginning of its second centenary.

2 The Labour Question

Globalization and the changing nature of work and work organization have challenged national industrial relations systems and diminished the power of social partners. Ongoing development has strongly affected collective bargaining regimes and altered their nature. At the same time, the traditional regulatory approaches of labour law have been challenged even more broadly, as managing changes in working life—caused, *inter alia*, by globalization, migration, an ageing workforce, urbanization, platformization, digitalization, climate change, and, most recently, the covid-19 pandemic—poses a central dilemma to national systems that were originally built for a more stable labour market. Importantly, the interplay between industrial relations and collective bargaining is undergoing complex change.[7]

Managing changes in working life caused by globalization poses a central challenge to labour law.[8] Protecting workers has become more difficult in a globalized world but there appears to be something even more fundamental in this dilemma: it is as if the understanding of those in need of protection offered by labour law would not be enough to produce socially just outcomes.[9] The dilemma could be illustrated with some observations of narratives that demonstrate the legal landscape where national labour law systems navigate.

The idea of embracing flexibility as a regulatory pattern in labour law involves a narrative of economic demands-based regulatory approaches meeting the needs of companies but increasingly also of individuals who are willing and capable to exercise their autonomy in building their jobs and careers. States have increasingly begun to make more room for individual autonomy when developing regulatory strategies that aim at more flexible labour standards and bargaining regimes that favour local level solutions. These developments involve regulatory solutions that do not necessarily undermine the worker-protective dimension of labour law but are coupled with it in the search for better employability and labour resilience. However, in several labour law systems, striving towards greater flexibility has come to signal

[7] See Liukkunen (2019a), p. 6.

[8] See Liukkunen (2005).

[9] See Langille (2018), pp. 101–103.

a strong individualization trend in regulation with adverse consequences for labour protection.[10]

Competition between states has advocated labour law reforms that pursue, to a variable extent, less binding regulation and more investment-friendly regulatory regimes. Importantly, economic considerations tend to be highlighted when seeking responses to globalization through adjustments to collective bargaining regimes. As a result, regulatory strategies that collective bargaining has traditionally offered in terms of developing social cohesion and equal labour standards are given more limited room.[11]

In its core, the labour question has been traditionally connected to unequal bargaining power and the need to level the imbalance between employer and employee.[12] However, this point of departure is becoming too narrow and is increasingly seen as demonstrating the rigidity of the limits of labour law. From the perspective of vulnerabilities, another perspective can be presented on the labour question. This tells a narrative where individuals do not determine their own path but are trapped in adverse conditions.[13] While flexibility is often pictured as being associated with freedom, capability, individual choices and future prospects, vulnerability looms in the context of the past and burdening, or exploitation, something to be managed or eliminated. Migrant and posted workers are vulnerable groups throughout the global labour market but there is also structural vulnerability that has to do with choices of exclusion and inclusion in the decisive regulatory frameworks.[14]

Globally, working life is characterized by a widening divide between those being protected and those not. The need to pay heed to those who require protection beyond the constellation of an employment contract means a need to identify development trends that do not become visible from the regulatory *façade* of societies. Two billion workers are working in the informal economy.[15] Although there is diversity in the circumstances of these workers, many lack decent working conditions. The narrative of vulnerabilities is pointing to a growing gap in the socio-economic position of individuals. Globalization has furthered problems relating to transnational social dumping, and the labour dimension of human trafficking still remains largely unidentified.[16] With forms of exploitation that do not have national borders,

[10] Liukkunen (2019a).

[11] See Ibid., p. 40.

[12] As characterized, "[t]he main object of labour law has always been, and we venture to say will always be, to be a countervailing force to counteract the inequality of bargaining power which is inherent and must be inherent in the employment relationship". See Davies and Freedland (1983), p. 18.

[13] The complexity of the dilemma of migration in relation to labour law has been observed, *inter alia*, by Costello and Freedland (2014).

[14] On patterns of social exclusion and inclusion see, for example, Carr and Chen (2004). On migrant workers' regulatory dilemma see Wolff (2018); and on posted workers' regulatory dilemma see Chen and Liukkunen (2019).

[15] See ILO (2018), p. 13.

[16] See for example, ILO (2020) demonstrating this. See also ILO (2017).

the narrative of vulnerabilities makes more inclusive regulatory responses highly significant to the ILO as an organization whose purpose is to promote social justice universally.[17]

3 Labour Law and Its Embedded Normativities

For the standard-setting work conducted by the ILO, it is not a matter of indifference how we define labour law issues and on what foundations the protective sphere of labour standards is being set in state systems of labour law.[18] In this sense, Western conceptions of labour law have not been fully at ease with the ILO in its global endeavours. First of all, labour law is traditionally a very domestically oriented field of law, featuring domestically oriented actors, policy objectives and interests. There is a broad consensus on the diversity of regulatory models employed in different countries. This has emphasized the contextuality of national labour law models in different economic and social settings.

Secondly, there are differences between labour law systems that easily become visible in comparative enquiries and mark different orientations to some basic questions of labour law. The difference between collective autonomy and contractual autonomy marks a noteworthy division of labour law approaches in domestic settings. While the first highlights collective bargaining, the second places an employment contract in the central position.[19] Collective bargaining is a cornerstone of several European labour law models, and the UK model shows itself as resting on contractual autonomy, with the legal role of collective agreements remaining voluntary.[20]

Along with well-established individual and collective dimensions, labour law has what could be characterized as a normative-institutional dimension illustrating labour market mechanisms that rest on particular institutional settings.[21] Their mutual connectivity and their influence on norm creation and enforcement is—in many countries—highly significant. As a public law-related enterprise, labour law highlights institutional conditions for developing workers' protection. It further emphasizes maintaining social peace and stability as important goals for social dialogue. Each dimension of labour law carries a systematic value but they can also be claimed to demonstrate embedded normativities which manifest themselves in legal practices highlighting the importance of viewing together substantive and

[17] See also Scelle (1930), p. 31.

[18] See also Langille (2019a), p. 508.

[19] See also Bogg et al. (2015), p. 4.

[20] See also Collins (2015).

[21] It should be noted that each division of labour law into different branches is shaped by legal-cultural characteristics. Even where the often used basic division of labour law into individual and collective is accepted, there is variation in the meaning content given.

procedural aspects of protection of workers.[22] The latter aspect relates to legal regimes as enabling workers to choose to use their collective rights or not.[23]

For the ILO, all this poses a demand to adopt a carefully composed picture of labour law which is necessary to approaching and explaining labour market phenomena without setting aside contextual nuances and underpinning values. The capability to speak the language of labour law has influenced not only the success of regulatory strategy but also the gradually developed working methods of the organization. To establish international labour standards, national diversity has required a particular sensitivity from the ILO as a regulator. An unspoken prerequisite has been to build the standard-setting work from the beginning on a strong tripartite basis and also to involve labour market parties in monitoring work.

The picture of labour law would remain incomplete if an approach based on labour rights were not to be noted. It is often emphasized that freedom of association requires particular attention within this frame.[24] For the ILO, the labour rights frame has provided an essential point of departure. The norm-setting structure of the ILO, together with its system of international labour standards, has heightened the special weight of social dialogue and collective bargaining, which forms an integral part of freedom of association, as highlighted by the ILO Constitution.[25]

The Philadelphia Declaration, as a part of the ILO Constitution, sets out the obligation to further effective recognition of the right of collective bargaining.[26] In the field of collective bargaining, too, the ILO approach has been characterized by noting the diversity of national models that can build collective voice and capacity. Yet, at the same time, the organization has been clear with the key components of the

[22] Tuori makes a useful distinction between law and legal practices. See Tuori (2016), p. 6, where legal practices are defined as social practices specialized in the production and reproduction of law.

[23] See also Langille (2018), p. 94, emphasizing the essence of the external legal structures labour law provides to bargaining regimes.

[24] See Bogg (2015), p. 105.

[25] See Constitution of the ILO which was adopted by the Peace Conference in April 1919, and became Part XIII of the Treaty of Peace of Versailles (28 June 1919). The Constitution has been amended in 1922, 1945, 1953, 1962, 1972, 1986 and 1997.

[26] Several ILO conventions and recommendations of the ILO concern collective bargaining. See Convention concerning Freedom of Association and Protection of the Right to Organise (No. 87) adopted on 17 June 1948; Convention concerning the Application of the Principles of the Right to Organise and to Bargain Collectively (No. 98) adopted on 8 June 1949; Declaration on Fundamental Principles and Rights at Work. Adopted by the International Labour Conference, 86th Session, Geneva, 18 June 1998 (Annex revised 15 June 2010); Collective Agreements Recommendation (No. 91) adopted on 29 June 1951; Convention concerning Protection and Facilities to be Afforded to Workers' Representatives in the Undertaking (No. 135) adopted on 23 June 1971; Voluntary Conciliation and Arbitration Recommendation (No. 92) adopted on 29 June 1951; Rural Workers' Organisations Recommendation (No. 149) adopted on 23 June 1975; Convention concerning Protection of the Right to Organise and Procedures for Determining Conditions of Employment in the Public Service (No. 151) adopted 27 June 1978; Labour Relations (Public Service) Recommendation (No. 159) adopted on 27 June 1978; Convention concerning the promotion of collective bargaining (No. 154) adopted on 19 June 1981; Collective Bargaining Recommendation (No. 163) adopted on 19 June 1981.

right to bargain and the requirements to be set to the autonomous framework of bargaining. Although standard-setting work of the ILO involves issues that raise different opinions among the ILO member states and the social partners, the strength of the ILO's approach has been connected to tripartite co-operation, which has made states and labour market organizations work together for certain goals.

In essence, the vitality of the system of international labour standards is dependent on the way the core area of labour rights is defined and spelled out by the ILO. Although the ILO is a central builder of minimum protection for workers, the deepest layer deriving from the Constitution of the organization binds together rights at work and social development. In this pursuit, international labour standards that protect freedom, equality and safety of workers are associated strongly with legal action against any injustice at work. Lately, this approach has gained a reinforced global perspective.

4 The ILO Vision of Decent Work: An Inclusive View of Work

The concepts of employee and contract of employment are used in different ways by domestic labour law systems in defining the scope of application of labour standards and highlighting the special nature of the relationship between employer and employee. However, as globalization has led to an increase in forms of work that are not covered by traditional labour law, the fact that work is increasingly carried out in diverse ways that fall between the spheres of work in an employment relationship and work as an independent entrepreneur has made connecting the idea of protection with a certain pre-determined legal status inadequate. Moreover, globally, forms of work that stand outside the official systems of societies constitute a largening group beyond any formal groupings.[27] Informal work is a significant form of employment, particularly in developing countries.[28]

As labour law with its protective elements has been unable to keep up with the changes in ways of working, a large number of workers have become unprotected. Workers in different positions share the same vulnerabilities.[29] As the ILO Constitution states that labour conditions must be improved, this requirement is not dependent on the form of work, be it work in an employment relationship or some other way of working.

Decent work, originally introduced by ILO Director-General Juan Somavia at the International Labour Conference in 1999, covers non-employment contract-based forms of work and work in the unofficial sector.[30] When Somavia introduced

[27] See ILO (2001, 2002a).

[28] See Daza (2005), where diversity of approaches to informal economy and its conceptualization as well as diverse treatment of informality are pointed out.

[29] See Davidov (2002), p. 417.

[30] See ILO (1999a).

the concept of decent work in the ILO it was constructed from four strategic objectives: promotion of rights at work; employment; social protection; and social dialogue.[31] From the beginning, there was an emphasis on the mutual interconnectivity between these objectives.

As far back as 2000 the ILO began a programme on decent work to pioneer ways in which decent work can be effectively promoted and applied in ILO member countries.[32] Two years later, a pilot programme was initiated for integrating decent work into the poverty reduction framework.[33] These moves were followed by an expansion of measures which manifested the centrality of the decent work agenda to the ILO as a means of renewal and modernization.

The decent work concept emphasizes that the social rights of labour are universal.[34] While highlighting this, the ILO can be read to affirm that the mechanisms of traditional labour law are alone insufficient to tackle the labour question in an inclusive way. Importantly, equality efforts behind the concept of decent work are based on the idea that employment cannot be separated from the quality of work.[35]

The ILO World Commission on the Social Dimension of Globalization adopted the idea of decent work as the basis of its proposals, and initiated decent work as the global goal of the multilateral system.[36] The report of the World Commission, issued in 2004, is written in the spirit of the Philadelphia Declaration.[37] The report reiterated the same concerns that were raised when the ILO was being founded and that can be found in its Constitution—poverty and inadequate labour conditions—and affirmed the importance of increasing the ILO's authority as a way of managing globalization.[38]

According to the World Commission, the management of globalization requires procedures that promote relating economic growth more closely with social progress and sustainable development.[39] The Commission paid critical attention to the imbalance in the world economy resulting from a fundamental imbalance between the economy, society, and polity. To correct this imbalance, the Commission stated that better institutional frameworks and policies are required. In particular, the imbalance between the economy and society has a detrimental effect on social justice. Global rules are not balanced because economic rules and institutions are stronger than social rules and institutions.[40]

---

[31] Ibid.

[32] The eight countries selected for the Programme were Bahrain, Bangladesh, Denmark, Ghana, Kazakhstan, Morocco, Panama and the Philippines. See ILO (n.d.-b).

[33] Awad (2005), para 4.

[34] See also Hepple (2002), pp. 255–256.

[35] See ILO (1999a).

[36] See World Commission on the Social Dimension of Globalization (2004), p. ix.

[37] The spirit of the Philadelphia Declaration of 1944 is often recalled by labour law scholars. See also Supiot (2012).

[38] See World Commission on the Social Dimension of Globalization (2004). See also ILO (2004).

[39] See World Commission on the Social Dimension of Globalization (2004), p. 2.

[40] See Ibid., pp. 3–4.

The most important task of the World Commission was to suggest concrete measures for managing the social dimension of globalization. The central vision of the Commission was a globalization process that would put people first, respect human dignity and consider everyone equal.[41] The Commission report highlights that the basic principles which must guide globalization are democracy, social equity, respect for human rights and the rule of law. Importantly, the Commission's labour-related proposals emphasize the objective of decent work for all as a global point of departure. They also highlight core labour standards as the minimum set of rules for which respect should be strengthened in all countries.[42]

The World Commission pointed out four factors that together form the concept of decent work. These are full employment, social protection, fundamental rights at work and social dialogue. According to the Commission, the concept of decent work is based on the idea that the development of social and labour policies requires a balance between employee protection, job creation, and competitiveness.[43]

Before conceptualization of decent work, which has become central to ILO globalization policy, the strategy of the ILO rested on a different scheme which highlighted perspectives deriving from Western-embedded labour law settings that focus on employment contracts and their regulatory frame. With decent work, the ILO adopted an inclusive view of work, a view stemming from its Constitution.[44] In so doing, the organization stressed the need to develop social and economic systems that guarantee basic security and employment but that also adjust to rapidly changing circumstances in a global market. The decent work agenda of the ILO builds on four pillars: (1) employment promotion, (2) social protection, (3) social dialogue and (4) rights at work. A synthetic perspective on the pillars has been strongly advocated by the ILO.[45]

The Declaration on Social Justice for Fair Globalization of 2008 was the outcome of tripartite consultations that began in the wake of the Report of the World Commission on the Social Dimension of Globalization. The Declaration institutionalized the decent work agenda, placing it at the core of the ILO's efforts to reach its constitutional objectives. Freedom of association and effective recognition of the right to collective bargaining were held as particularly important to enable realization of decent work.[46]

---

[41] See Ibid., pp. 5–6.

[42] See Ibid, p. 55, 91 and 110.

[43] See Ibid., pp. 64–67 and pp. 108–114.

[44] The Philadelphia Declaration of 1944, which forms an essential part of the ILO Constitution, extended the work of the ILO by stating that all human beings, irrespective of race, creed or sex, have the right to pursue both their material well-being and their spiritual development in conditions of freedom and dignity, of economic security and equal opportunity. It stated that the attainment of the conditions in which this shall be possible must constitute the central aim of national and international policy. See also Article 23 of the Universal Declaration of Human Right. Adopted by the United Nations General Assembly, 3rd Session, Paris, 10 December 1948.

[45] See also ILO (1999b).

[46] Preface to the ILO Declaration on Social Justice for a Fair Globalization. Adopted by the International Labour Conference, 97th Session, Geneva, 10 June 2008.

In the UN 2030 Agenda for Sustainable Development, decent work is one of the indivisible sustainable development goals (SDGs), formulated as "Decent work and economic growth". The wording of SDG 8 does not correspond to the ILO original point of departure and the goal of decent work was included in the Millenium Development Targets only in 2005. For the ILO, SDG 8 is, however, an achievement based on its efforts to have decent work adopted in the 2030 Agenda.[47] Importantly, the idea of inclusivity was placed at the heart of sustainability. The UN targets for SDG 8 do not completely correspond to the decent work agenda of the ILO, and the perspective on fundamental labour rights advocated by the ILO would require broader attention.[48] However, the UN 2030 Agenda has turned out in many ways important to the ILO, offering a longed-for opportunity to strengthen the position of the organization within the UN system.

With decent work, the ILO has gained a new voice within the UN system and the international multilateral system more generally. Thus, at the beginning of its second centenary the organization has acquired an opportunity to build more authority on its renewed character of global orientation. While the decent work agenda has gradually grown to renew the way of approaching the labour question in the regulatory strategy of the ILO, it can be seen as having potential to reinforce the global role of the organization. In essence, decent work as an objective rejects the narrow conceptual frame of traditional labour law, reminding us that labour law cannot be far from any groups of working individuals.

The ILO Centenary Declaration for the Future of Work of 2019 constructs a commitment to decent work and sustainability by linking social, trade, financial, economic and environmental policies together. It states that the ILO must move forward into its second century by further developing its human-centred approach to the future of work, which puts workers' rights and the rights of all people at the heart of economic, social and environmental policies. Moreover, it highlights the decent work agenda.[49] However, there seems to be a need for a perspective of broader interconnections between decent work and climate change within the sustainable development framework under construction. Although the ILO Guidelines for a just transition towards environmentally sustainable economies and societies for all,[50] issued in 2015, present several ways of reinforcing these interconnections and "just transition" has been adopted as an objective of the ILO policy efforts towards sustainability, there would be a need for further elaboration.[51] It is to be noted that the environmental perspective on SDG 8 is also still under

---

[47] See Frey and MacNaughton (2016), pp. 2–3.

[48] See UN (n.d.). On the other hand, although the decent work agenda governs only core labour standards explicitly, several ILO conventions relate to and support the agenda. See also MacNaughton and Frey (2011), p. 446.

[49] See ILO, Centenary Declaration for the Future of Work. Adopted by the International Labour Conference, 108th Session, Geneva, 21 June 2019.

[50] See ILO (2015).

[51] See also Doorey (2017), Doorey (2015), pp. 560–563.

construction.[52] There appears to be a need for a broader approach which puts weight on a decent life as a frame for decent work to assess and alter societal processes that hinder humane conditions of work.

5 Fundamental Labour Rights: Tasks Ahead

Fundamental labour rights, or core labour standards, form a central pillar of the concept of decent work.[53] They also integrate decent work in the core of the system of international labour standards. The decent work agenda highlights social dialogue and collective labour rights in dealing with inequalities.[54] On this view, the demand for decency derives from the demand for democracy and participation, aligning with the ILO Constitution.

However, efforts surrounding the definition, goals, and content of the core standards were originally met with considerable international debate and controversy, which lasted until the end of the 1990s. Prior to the definition of core labour standards in the 1998 ILO Declaration on Fundamental Principles and Rights at Work,[55] a lack of clarity existed as to standards that could be considered central labour standards and whose global implementation should be promoted.

A central starting point for the 1998 Declaration was the UN World Summit for Social Development in Copenhagen in 1995. The Summit was the first time the social dimension of globalization was discussed at the highest political level. It approved the Copenhagen Declaration on Social Development and Programme of Action where governments agreed to promote the fundamental rights of employees. These were based on the central ILO conventions and included forced and child labour bans, freedom of association, collective bargaining rights, the principle of equal treatment of men and women, and a ban on discrimination.[56] It was the first time the content of core labour standards was defined on the basis of the central ILO conventions. The Summit followed the first WTO Ministerial Meeting held in Singapore in 1996, which also played an important role in the development. The Meeting approved the Singapore Ministerial Declaration containing a commitment to observe internationally recognized core labour standards. The Declaration also expressed the WTO's approval of the ILO's activities and accepted that preparing international core labour

[52] See for example the outcome of Weitz et al. (2019) pointing to difficulties of individual states in gaining an understanding of the environmental issues under SDG 8.

[53] See Javillier (2003), p. 3.

[54] See also Moreau (2013).

[55] ILO, Declaration on Fundamental Principles and Rights at Work. Adopted by the International Labour Conference, 86th Session, Geneva, 18 June 1998 (Annex revised 15 June 2010).

[56] See in more detail Copenhagen Declaration on Social Development and Programme of Action of the World Summit for Social Development 1995.

standards fell under the ILO's authority.[57] It brought clarity to the role of the ILO and included clear approval by the WTO of core labour standards.[58]

The Declaration of the WTO Meeting in Singapore formed a central source in preparing the ILO Declaration on Fundamental Principles and Rights at Work, indeed affecting its content. The ILO Declaration was approved at the 86th Session of the International Labour Conference in 1998 and the content of core labour standards was exactly the same as when they were defined for the first time at the Copenhagen Summit. Essentially, the core labour standards were a development which followed the 1996 WTO ministerial meeting in Singapore, where it was affirmed that the ILO is the competent body to set and deal with these standards. The four principles in the 1998 ILO Declaration, generally referred to as fundamental labour rights or core labour standards, are: (1) freedom of association and collective bargaining, (2) prohibition of forced labour, (3) elimination of child labour and (4) non-discrimination in employment. These core labour standards are included in a total of eight ILO conventions also referred to as the core or key conventions.[59]

The ILO Declaration transformed the way labour rights are viewed internationally although there has not been consensus on what this has meant in legal terms.[60] Core labour standards are considered to be binding on ILO member states directly on the basis of the ILO Constitution and the principles of these standards are included in several international human rights conventions. The monitoring of core conventions that core labour standards derive from differs from that of other conventions in that reports must be produced on core conventions annually, while most of the other conventions are reported on once every five years. The Declaration on Fundamental Principles and Rights at Work introduced the Follow-up procedure that promotes implementation of core labour standards and involves regular reports on the implementation of ratified conventions as well as a complaints procedure based on the ILO Constitution. In addition, reports are requested every year from countries that have not ratified the core conventions. The Declaration aims to take

[57] See WTO, Singapore Ministerial Declaration, adopted on 13 December 1996. See also Fields (2003), p. 65.

[58] See Leary (1997), p. 1.

[59] These conventions are the Convention concerning Freedom of Association and Protection of the Right to Organise (No. 87) adopted on 17 June 1948; the Convention concerning the Application of the Principles of the Right to Organise and to Bargain Collectively (No. 98) adopted on 8 June 1949; the Convention concerning Forced or Compulsory Labour (No. 29) adopted on 10 June 1930 (and its of 2014 to the Forced Labour Convention adopted on 28 May 2014); the Convention concerning the Abolition of Forced Labour (No. 105) adopted on 5 June 1957; the Convention concerning Minimum Age for Admission to Employment (No. 138) adopted on 6 June 1973; the Convention concerning the Prohibition and Immediate Action for the Elimination of the Worst Forms of Child Labour (No. 182) adopted on 1 June 1999; the Convention concerning Equal Remuneration for Men and Women Workers for Work of Equal Value (No. 100) adopted on 6 June 1951; the Convention concerning Discrimination in Respect of Employment and Occupation (No. 111) adopted 4 June 1958.

[60] See for example Alston (2004), pp. 457–521 for the characteristics of the well-known scholarly criticism of core labour standards.

into consideration difficulties for developing countries to adopt international core labour standards on account of their lower stage of economic development. It stresses that core labour standards must not be used for promoting protectionist financial goals and that the Declaration must not be appealed to for such purposes.

Great economic, social and political differences of countries have had an impact on attitudes towards core labour standards, which have also been criticized for being too narrow in content and because concentrating on them can mean disregard for other central labour standards.[61] Often, occupational health and safety have been highlighted as issues that would require priority along with the core standards. Although the absence of health and safety from core labour standards poses a difficulty, the linkage between collective labour rights and health and safety should be noted.

Collective labour rights build on capacities and participatory mechanisms that are important for ensuring safety and health at work. In addition to social dialogue at the workplace level, employee participation rights, information and consultation, contribute to developing health and safety. Health and safety management can be supported by an efficient employee participation system. The central idea behind collective labour rights is that they carry in them a capacity building character which enables regulatory development towards fairer terms and secure conditions of work.[62] The influence of collective labour rights thus also highlights their relation to other labour standards.[63]

ILO Conventions Nos. 87 (freedom of association and the right to organise) and 98 (collective bargaining) set together the fundamental frame for collective labour rights. The evolution of the number of ratifications of core conventions, however, shows that significant progress is lacking in their adoption and recent regulatory development has also posed problems to these two conventions. To illustrate, the workforce of countries that have not ratified Convention No. 87 amounts to over 1.55 billion workers, and Convention No. 98 over 1.49 billion workers. Generally, protection of the right of freedom of association and collective bargaining has declined in recent decades.[64] Notably, this kind of development is also visible in countries that have ratified these two core conventions.[65]

Adoption of the decent work agenda and the related strategy shift of the ILO can be seen as a kind of response to weak recognition of core labour standards and the relatively low number of ratifications of the recent ILO conventions.[66] Even when conventions have been ratified, their enforcement has often been viewed inadequate. The 1998 Declaration is premised on the idea that core labour standards are global and they have been formulated to the effect that they can be universally applied.

---

[61] See for example Alston and Heenan (2004).

[62] See ILO (2002b).

[63] Ibid., p. vi.

[64] See ILO (n.d.-a).

[65] See Liukkunen (2019a). See also Marx et al. (2015).

[66] As regards most recent conventions, the number of ratifications can be found at ILO (n.d.-a).

The development of ratifications of ILO core conventions raises a need to call for a more precise account of fundamental rights development, aligning it to the broader frame of labour market and societal changes in each country. One could also ask whether the perspective that is traditionally offered to an assessment of the influence of fundamental labour rights on national labour law regimes needs complementing. A broader perspective would bring together different actors as participants of legal practices: legislatures, labour inspectorates, courts and arbitration committees as well as various non-state actors that shape and foster space for the evolution of labour rights in different and differentiated legal and societal contexts of work.[67] There are countries that despite non-ratification of core conventions, often with long-term country-specific technical assistance from the ILO, strive towards developing their laws to meet the core labour standards. On a broader view, the effects of international labour standards can be found at different layers of normativity, which highlights interaction, dialogue and mutual enforcement.[68]

Of the UN organizations, the ILO is unique in its tripartite nature. This adds special weight to the organization's standard-setting work and monitoring mechanism.[69] Throughout its history, the ILO has carried out its work in different kinds of situations where the co-operation model has been put to the test. A recent development posing a new kind of challenge to the ILO comes from outside the classic labour standard-setting paradigm. This concerns a need to take a stand towards new regulatory actors entering the international labour standard-setting arena. The ILO is present in a supportive role in the social development of individual countries, but its authority and presence would also be required in transnational regulatory settings where new labour standards are being created—often with remarkable speed and intensity. There is a need to more firmly anchor respect for fundamental labour rights to the area of cross-border privatization of labour law. The question of effective incorporation of core labour standards into transnational sets of labour standards created by various non-state actors has become increasingly central in terms of labour protection and the social dimension of globalization. While promoting ratification of ILO conventions follows well-established operational modes, promoting transnational incorporation of core labour standards takes the ILO into unknown regulatory terrain. Yet the voice and authority of the ILO is needed in regulatory contexts where international actors independently organize and create new sets of rules of labour governance to ensure that the labour rights-based perspective is not sidelined.

---

[67] See an analysis of ways to approach the question of implementing international labour standards from a legal-cultural perspective, Liukkunen and Chen (2016), pp. 6–9.

[68] See Liukkunen (2019a), p. 10.

[69] See also in this volume Waas (2020).

6 Collective Bargaining and Changing Regulatory Frames

Freedom of association and right to collective bargaining are facing challenges that derive from both international and domestic regulatory settings.[70] Developments in the EU point to the vulnerability of domestic collective bargaining regimes along with a certain undermining of the right to exercise collective rights. There are many approaches to labour law in the EU, and the expansion of substantive EU labour legislation has improved labour protection in many central issues. However, as strong economic integration has been held as vital to the competitiveness of the internal market and EU Member States, it has resulted in overriding the respect for fundamental labour rights and values in the context of cross-border employment when the exercise of EU fundamental economic freedoms is involved. In the *Viking* and *Laval* cases, the CJEU handed down controversial judgments that demonstrate a tension between the right to collective bargaining, or the right to industrial action, on the one hand, and EU fundamental economic freedoms, on the other.[71] These judgments inaugurated a new era of fundamental labour rights in the EU. Although the EU Charter of Fundamental Rights protects the right to bargain collectively, together with the right to industrial action, in these CJEU judgments collective labour rights have been subjected to certain limitations in a cross-border setting when fundamental economic freedoms are at stake but without a clear constitutional basis for this. The practice of the ILO supervisory organs does not recognize the type of discretion that the CJEU has applied in its jurisprudence concerning the conditions set to the right to take industrial action.[72]

CJEU jurisprudence in the *Laval Quartet* has been challenging in terms of the workers' human rights commitments of the EU Member States.[73] Significantly, from the 1990s onwards, the ECtHR has developed the protective nature of the European Human Rights Convention and increasingly extended protection of the principles of the Convention to govern collective labour rights. To some extent, this has offered a counterforce to the destabilization of the protective framework of cross-border collective labour rights caused by the jurisprudence of the CJEU. In *Demir and Baykara*, the ECtHR confirmed that Article 11 of the ECHR governs the right to collective bargaining.[74]

---

[70] Chapters 6 and 7 of this article draw partially on the author's research published in Liukkunen (2019b).

[71] CJEU (Grand Chamber), *Laval un Partneri Ltd v Svenska Byggnadsarbetareförbundet, Svenska Byggnadsarbetareförbundets avdelning 1, Byggettan and Svenska Elektrikerförbundet* (Case C-341/05), Judgment, 18 December 2007; CJEU (Grand Chamber), *International Transport Workers' Federation and Finnish Seamen's Union v Viking Line ABP and OÜ Viking Line Eesti* (Case C-438/05), Judgment, 11 December 2007.

[72] See ILO Committee of Experts (2010), p. 209.

[73] The Laval quartet constitutes of CJEU judgments Viking and Laval as well as CJEU (Second Chamber), *Dirk Rüffert v Land Niedersachsen* (Case C-346/06), Judgment, 3 April 2008; and CJEU (First Chamber) Commission of the European Communities v Grand Duchy of Luxemburg (Case C-319/06), Judgment, 19 June 2008.

[74] See European Court of Human Rights (Grand Chamber), *Demir and Baykara v. Turkey* (App. No. 34503/97), Judgment, 12 November 2008.

Moreover, recent development of domestic collective bargaining regimes is highly significant in terms of understanding the pressing challenges of labour law. Strong centralized collective bargaining systems are traditionally considered as a Continental and Nordic European phenomenon. There are also well-established systems based on decentralized bargaining, like those of North America and Japan. Importantly, each collective bargaining model should be seen in the context of the country's labour rights status.[75] Although the right to collective bargaining enjoys constitutional recognition in several national legal systems this does not necessarily translate into heightened protection.

The challenge of combining flexibility and safety penetrates collective bargaining systems, and related balancing efforts have increasingly often unravelled to the benefit of flexibility. A shift towards more local level bargaining has been simultaneously occurring in many bargaining systems. Yet decentralization has occurred within remarkably diverse regulatory frameworks with different emphases and divergent locally-embedded solutions.[76] In some countries, centralized models of collective bargaining have increasingly been replaced by decentralized ones, whereas in others the national or sectoral level still plays a key coordinative role.

Increasing pressure towards greater flexibility and tensions between flexibility and security appear common to bargaining systems worldwide. Mandatory minimum protection of workers has been weakened in both systems that are decentralized by nature and systems that have become increasingly decentralized.[77] Several development trends are reshaping the subject matter of collective bargaining and narrow the protective sphere of collective agreements. Also the role of minimum protection afforded by the system of general applicability of collective agreements (*erga omnes*) in some states has been affected.

Several countries have altered their regulatory approach to collective bargaining in a situation where union density is declining and the coverage of collective agreements is diminishing. The hierarchy between collective agreements at different levels has changed and decentralization of bargaining structures has become a significant regulatory objective for many national legislatures. Opportunities to deviate from labour legislation and from upper level collective agreements have been enabled to a larger extent by local agreements. This has brought about new kind of local labour governance models.

There are national legislatures that have actively sought to promote flexibilization and decentralization of the collective agreement system through reforms that touch upon the core area of collective autonomy. In some cases the reforms have resulted in tension between sectoral or branch level and local level agreements, especially when strengthening the status of local level agreements at the cost of higher level agreements and their coordinative function has been sought. In addition, *in peius* deviations from mandatory labour legislation or higher level collective

[75] See Liukkunen (2019a), pp. 4–5.

[76] See Ibid., p. 5.

[77] See Ibid.

agreements by local agreements have been enabled or expanded in some countries.[78] To a notable extent this has occurred against the legal tradition and basic labour law principles of these countries.[79]

Even when local agreements are concluded on the basis of the competence conferred by a sectoral collective agreement, local agreements may lead to highly differentiated rules between companies. Differentiation, which may continue within individual companies, treats issues that are traditionally regulated by collective agreements very differently. In some issues benefits can be reaped while in others a broader regulatory frame could be necessary.[80] In some countries, decentralization has been partial and gradual and based on well-established tripartite law drafting processes whereas in others less balanced processes and outcomes have undermined the role of social dialogue. On the other hand, decentralization can be seen not only as a result of legislative reforms, but also of decreasing trade union density, changes in the power balance of bargaining and overall weakening of the role of the social partners. But in some cases, as the post-socialist countries in Eastern Europe demonstrate, it can also be given particular historical explanations.[81]

6.1 *Individualization in Decentralization of Collective Bargaining*

The individualization trend in labour law is often offered with an explanation which relates to economically indispensable efforts to meet the needs of companies and individual workers, albeit from different angles. For companies, flexibility in different forms has become essential to ensure continuity of business and change management, and the increase of regulative flexibility is rooted in this demand. Workers' perspective involves a broad range of issues including the influence of the spread of atypical employment. While a more individualistic regulatory approach relates to growing flexibility, there is a growing number of new categories of workers whose position differs from that of a traditional employee. Different and differentiated groups of non-standard workers tend to have less bargaining power, but they may also have less opportunities of attending to collective efforts to improve labour standards. Although evidence is available that in some countries social dialogue involves developing new strategies to improve protection of atypical work, the transformation of work is so profound that it adds pressure to adopt more inclusive bargaining frameworks.[82]

---

[78] See for example Kun (2019), Magnani (2019) and Mazuyer (2019).

[79] See Liukkunen (2019a), pp. 16–20.

[80] The ILO (2002b) points to the relevance of the level of bargaining in terms of health and safety issues. While much of the capacity building of health and safety protection occurs at the enterprise level, there are issues of health and safety where a national or sectoral level regulatory framework is needed to ensure necessary protection.

[81] See Liukkunen (2019a), pp. 7–9.

[82] Ibid., p. 54.

The development of bargaining regimes in the direction of more flexibility is creating new kinds of vulnerabilities. Decentralization leads to situations where issues that previously were negotiated between collective actors are increasingly decided between employer and employee at the workplace level. Individualized bargaining agendas reflect a growing emphasis on the employer–employee relationship in decollectivization of labour law. Local bargaining is increasingly enabling differentiation of the terms of employment on the basis of the needs of individual companies. As a result, locally bargained rules are more individualized than those in higher level agreements.[83]

New patterns and methods of setting terms of employment are evolving at the local level in a way that highlights both local procedures and bargaining as an individualized process between employer and employee. As a result, the procedural protection offered by traditional means of collective bargaining systems is declining. Existing dispute resolution mechanisms are required to show adaptability in dealing with labour standards deriving from new kinds of contractual arrangements. While local bargaining allows much discretion, employees need procedural safeguards in order to ensure a sufficient balance of workplace-level negotiations.

It appears that the traditional mode of collective bargaining has lost sight of some aspects of the labour market change.[84] This change calls for developing institutional settings and local bargaining capacities to enable negotiations based on a more equal footing between the parties and it also calls for rethinking the substance. A clearer picture is needed of how local bargaining and employee participation could be integrated in order to advance the capacities of local bargaining. Connections which often exist between collective bargaining, on the one hand, and employee information and consultation, on the other, also speak for improving coverage of employee participation systems in terms of different forms of non-standard work.[85]

6.2 *Decollectivization of Industrial Relations*

In many bargaining systems, both decentralized and centralized, declining collective agreement coverage and union density as well as institutional and regulatory changes are driving towards decollectivization of industrial relations. Even where decentralization has been organized, notable changes have occurred in the institutional settings of bargaining frameworks. In some systems, the position of trade unions in local level bargaining has been weakened so that they can be bypassed when local agreements are negotiated.

[83] Ibid., p. 32.

[84] See also Estlund (2015), p. 260.

[85] Liukkunen (2019a), pp. 54–55.

Importantly, the interplay between industrial relations and collective bargaining is in the process of change. Well-established labour institutions have often had a multi-level impact on the development of labour standards not only within labour law regimes but also in making more room for a labour rights frame in societies. Often, long-term promotion of the interests of workers and bargaining have been required to enable the birth of the collective agreements, which have provided legally enforceable minimum standards. Today, decentralization decreases the bargaining power of trade unions which has built collective capacities in an evolutionary way.

Collective bargaining is increasingly understood as producing frameworks for individualized flexibility along with adjustments to labour standards required for ensuring employability, competitiveness and efficiency. At the local level, new patterns and methods of setting labour standards are evolving in a way which highlights employer discretion. These developments have occurred simultaneously with a certain polarization of labour markets. However, it should also be emphasized that the transformation of industrial relations which relates to decollectivization has occurred in various degrees and modes in different bargaining systems.[86]

6.3 The ILO and the Challenge of Decentralization

National regulatory frameworks which were originally built to enable and maintain autonomous collective bargaining within the framework of corporatist arrangements have been increasingly transformed into frameworks which not only coordinate and manage but also set limitations on collective bargaining. This change derives from economic considerations that align businesses interests and state regulatory approaches or, in the case of the EU, international institutions exercising financial power, as the experience of the European semester demonstrates. As a result, less inclusive and less protective collective bargaining regimes are emerging, highlighting the adaptability of labour and the adjustability of the system. To illustrate, austerity measures adopted within the economic governance model of the EU have influenced the regulatory framework of collective bargaining and labour standards, in particular in Mediterranean countries.[87] These measures have confronted a critical stand by the ILO Committee of Freedom of Association. In the case of Greece, the Committee noted significant interventions in the voluntary nature of collective bargaining and in the principle of the inviolability of freely concluded collective agreements.[88]

Some of the changes in collective bargaining regimes that we are witnessing derive from regulatory adaptation to profound changes in work while some come from a certain economization of labour law regimes. The scope and extent of

[86] See also Dukes (2014), p. 9.

[87] See Liukkunen (2019a), pp. 29–31; Seifert (2014).

[88] ILO Committee of Freedom of Association (2012), para 995.

protection that collective channels and institutions provide to workers are being challenged in ways that bear consequences for the protection of the rights of workers. In many countries, including those with well-established centralized or decentralized bargaining regimes, collective labour law mechanisms are in complex transition. The development of individualization and decollectivization appears distant from the original idea of collective bargaining related to workers' collective pursuit of labour rights. It can be argued that the pursuit of greater flexibility has come to undermine the labour rights perspective and values that are manifested in workplaces in the right to bargain collectively.

The principle of labour protection upon which labour law is built presupposes collective actors and institutions that can exercise collective power and pressure in order to manifest and defend the collective interest of workers. In essence, a set of key values, democracy, interest representation and autonomy, is involved.[89] However, it should be added that singling out and focusing on the collective interest is not alone enough to identify the labour question of our day. The regulatory framework for collective bargaining needs to be viewed from a broader perspective in search of a response to changes in the labour market. In the future, we may face new types of labour institutions or reformed institutions and regulatory frameworks that replace or complement those based on a more stable working life. Reforms are required to build legal-institutional space for the development of meaningful employee participation in our time and to achieve an adaptable system of labour governance. Reforms could also be called for in order to advocate regulatory models to tackle most pressing issues of inequality in novel ways. Collective bargaining regimes have tended to focus minor attention on some areas of labour law. They could assume a greater role in promoting gender equality and women's position in and contribution to the labour market, workers' employability and protection regardless of age, race or other categorizations as well as other issues where more effective safeguards would be necessary.[90]

When asking what role the ILO should assume in this particular transition context it has to be recalled that the organization is known for careful observance of working life development. It appears clear that the ILO is needed not only to speak for and explain the foundations of collective labour rights but also to increase our understanding of a normative development driven by changes in different regulatory surroundings with the broader labour rights scene in mind. The emphasis of social dialogue and collective labour rights has been central to understanding the well-being of workers as offered by the organization.

A deeper meaning of the right to collective bargaining in its distinctive characteristic is that it introduces collective enabling capacity to labour relations and development of labour standards.[91] The idea of labour protection as a collective phenomenon has been legitimizing the autonomy of collective bargaining and the social partners in their relation to the state. This, in turn, has shaped the strong status

[89] See Liukkunen (2019a), p. 60.

[90] See Ibid., p. 60.

[91] See also Langille (2019b).

of collective agreements in many labour law systems. What has happened recently is that labour governance has given way to economic governance. Adjustments to bargaining frameworks placing great importance on economic factors have narrowed the space of labour rights-oriented argumentation and values.[92] There is a need to reconnect the requirement of labour protection to economic performance and productivity in order to achieve a broader understanding of mutual connectivity.[93] This requires a deeper dialogue underlining the role of the ILO.

7 Transnational Dimension of Labour Protection

Some of the biggest challenges to labour law relate to the sway of its assumption of territoriality, which forces a broadening of horizons beyond domestically oriented considerations to transnational developments in labour law.[94] Actors such as international financial institutions have entered the arena of international labour standards creation, shaking traditional assumptions of regulatory power and authority. As a consequence, labour law has increasingly come to operate as transnational law beyond the traditional national—international labour law dichotomy, resulting in regulatory developments that both supplement and compete with traditional legal frameworks. Within transnational private regimes, labour rights are addressed in the context of self-governance and contractual arrangements that are not guided by public regulation. Private actors that lack a connection to the traditional system of international labour standards assume capability for shaping modes of labour standards within transnational normative frameworks where they would otherwise be absent.[95]

Globalization has raised several challenges for international labour law and poses a constant test of the legal applicability of international labour standards when multinational enterprises (MNEs) are operating on a transnational basis in various countries and regions. The regulatory framework of MNEs is manifold, consisting of multiple overlapping regimes with a reach broader than the law of national states. Important international documents providing guidelines for MNEs were already drawn up in the 1970s. A pioneer in providing guidelines for enterprises was the OECD, whose Guidelines were drawn to provide recommendations for MNEs and included in the Declaration on International Investment and Multinational Enterprises.[96] A year later, the ILO presented the Tripartite Declaration of Principles concerning Multinational Enterprises and Social Policy (MNE Declaration),[97] and

---

[92] Liukkunen (2019a), p. 54.

[93] See also in this volume Waas (2020).

[94] See Mundlak (2009).

[95] See Liukkunen (2014) pp. 163–167.

[96] See OECD, Declaration on International Investment and Multinational Enterprises. First adopted in 1976, and reviewed in 1979, 1984, 1991, 2000 and 2011.

[97] See ILO, Tripartite Declaration of Principles concerning Multinational Enterprises and Social Policy. Adopted by the Governing Body, 204th Session, Geneva, November 1977, and amended at

the UN launched negotiations for guidelines for MNEs.[98] At this stage, business was still largely considered to be a bipolar operation involving home and host states.

The second phase of laying down guidelines for MNEs, which began in the mid-1990s, stemmed from expanding globalization and the networking of business operations. Importantly, it was this phase that introduced the 1998 ILO Declaration and resolved the question of the content of core labour standards. The OECD published a widely revised version of its Guidelines in 2000 to match the ILO Declaration, and renewed the Guidelines again in 2011.[99] In the same year, the UN Guiding Principles on Business and Human Rights were adopted.[100] Later, core labour standards were included in the MNE Declaration and the incorporation of specific decent work issues occurred in 2017.[101] In recent years we have witnessed significant reformulations of MNEs' global production as well as a remarkable expansion of international documents that promote labour protection in the operations of MNEs. Today, all the major public international guidelines that seek to steer MNEs' behaviour recognize the status of ILO fundamental labour rights.[102]

However, the voluntary approach to labour rights suffers from weaknesses. Corporate codes of conduct rarely include full references to core labour standards despite multiple international efforts to reinforce them. Although they were included in the OECD Guidelines and in the ILO's MNE Declaration, we remain far from core labour standards forming the core of enterprise labour policies. The division of duties between states and MNEs as regards the execution of workers' rights has become one of the central questions in managing the social dimension of globalization.[103] As privatization of labour standard-making proceeds, an increasing need exists to find ways to place fundamental labour rights protection more directly at the core of corporate social responsibility (CSR). There is a need to concretize other aspects of the decent work agenda in the operations of MNEs as well.

7.1 *Transnational Collectivization of Labour Law*

Transnational labour law has broadened the spectrum of collective contractual arrangements that relate to promotion of labour protection. Previously the domestic nature of collective bargaining systems was emphasized, and questions concerning the cross-border dimension of collective agreements typically arose either when a

279th (November 2000), 295th (March 2006) and 329th (March 2017) Sessions.

[98] The outcome of the negotiations was a Draft United Nations Code of Conduct on Transnational Corporations. For more details, see Intergovernmental Working Group on a Code of Conduct (1982).

[99] See OECD (2011) OECD Guidelines for Multinational Enterprises. OECD Publishing, Paris.

[100] Human Rights Council (2011).

[101] See ILO, Tripartite Declaration of Principles concerning Multinational Enterprises and Social Policy. Adopted by the Governing Body, 204th Session, Geneva, November 1977, and amended at 279th (November 2000), 295th (March 2006) and 329th (March 2017) Sessions.

[102] See Liukkunen (2016), p. 157.

[103] See also ILO, OECD, IOM, UNICEF (2019), p. 1.

domestic collective agreement was made to concern work to be carried out abroad, or when the applicability of a domestic collective agreement to workers temporarily working abroad was to be resolved.[104]

Transnational agreements, falling outside the traditional categorizations and conceptualizations of labour law, are brought about within transnational normative frames that cross countries and regions. These agreements strive from certain normative-institutional settings of company-level industrial relations. Both international and domestic labour organizations as well as European Works Councils (EWCs) have been negotiating these agreements from the labour side with MNEs. Especially the role of EWCs, established in the EU countries on the basis of the EWC Directive[105] for transnational information and consultation of workers in large Community-scale undertakings and groups of undertakings, has become significant in paving the way for transnational contractual arrangements promoting labour rights.

Generally speaking, transnational company agreements (TCAs) encompass a variety of forms of agreement concluded between an MNE on the one side and international or national trade union federations or other parties representing employees on the other side. European TCAs, which normally apply to an MNE and its subsidiaries in the European countries where the multinational operates, typically reflect issues that are of concern in the European labour market, such as anticipating and managing social changes concerning restructuring.[106]

International framework agreements (IFAs), in turn, are a specific group of transnational agreements. They are concluded between an MNE and global union federations, and other parties such as an EWC or a global works council representing workers, with a global reach. Often, IFAs seek to ensure respect for ILO core labour standards in MNE operations in all the countries where the company operates. However, despite international efforts to advance broader applicability in the operations of MNEs, they frequently lack governance over company supply chains.

IFAs derive firstly from centralized negotiating processes, which are dependent on functioning social dialogue at the MNE level, and secondly from sufficiently balanced employee representation within MNEs. Concluding these agreements requires certain reorganization of the regulatory power of trade unions at transnational level. As they appear, IFAs conceptualize the transnational context of social dialogue, which significantly differs from contexts of national systems and balancing processes that lie behind collective bargaining in domestic settings.[107] From the perspective of workers' organizations, IFAs can be seen as strengthening not only industrial relations but also the global union federations themselves.[108] They have an

[104] See Liukkunen (2019a), p. 44.

[105] See Directive 2009/38/EC of the European Parliament and of the Council of 6 May 2009 on the establishment of a European Works Council or a procedure in Community-scale undertakings and Community-scale groups of undertakings for the purposes of informing and consulting employees (Recast).

[106] See Liukkunen (2019a), pp. 44–45.

[107] See also Liukkunen (2019a), p. 44.

[108] See Müller et al. (2008).

important role in shaping transnational industrial relations and social dialogue.[109] Altogether, transnational agreements can be viewed as offering a foundation for collectivization of labour law in a transnational setting.

Transnational agreements are not concluded in a void but in interaction with diverse normative regimes. This makes it important to pay heed to larger institutional and regulatory structures and their enabling character.[110] These agreements have grown out of a need to ensure compliance with certain labour standards and basic social values, but many other normative dimensions have remained underexplored. For example, the impact of the broader normative frameworks of corporate governance on transnational contractual commitments has remained a largely unexamined area.[111]

Another important issue is how diverse domestic regulatory frameworks of collective bargaining influence transnational negotiations. National collective bargaining systems may involve regulatory, structural or institutional constraints that restrict development of transnational contractual arrangements, as demonstrated by Brazilian experience of efforts to conclude a transnational agreement. In a case where an IFA was negotiated, Brazilian single trade union system, permitting only one trade union at each bargaining level, became a major obstacle to successful transnational negotiations until a contractual model to overcome this was developed.[112] The institutional bargaining frame at the national level may also influence the development of transnational negotiations so that transformation of labour unions is required. Japanese experience shows that a decentralized bargaining model of enterprise-based unions may affect entering into transnational negotiations so that transformation is required from industrial relations institutions to build transnational negotiating capacities.[113]

Several aspects of the content of IFAs deserve attention. In addition to focusing on fundamental labour rights, IFAs tackle other issues that are relevant to equality and expansion of substantive content of labour protection. They involve issues such as social dialogue, health and safety at work, career and skills development, training, anti-corruption, protection of personal data and internet policy. The expansion of labour issues governed is a noteworthy development in terms of labour standards coverage.

Although IFAs are associated with promotion of fundamental labour rights, the role of collective labour rights may be limited or absent. However, there is also evidence of opposite development. The first Spanish agreement covering a retail supply chain was the agreement between Inditex and IndustriAll Global Union, originally concluded in 2007.[114] The objective of the agreement, which was renewed

[109] See (2019a), pp. 44–49. See also Blasi and Bair (2019), p. 40; Papadakis et al. (2008), p. 85.

[110] See Liukkunen (2013).

[111] On the normative activities of multinationals and the legal environment thereto, see, Danielsen (2005), p. 412.

[112] See Maia (2019), p. 118.

[113] See Araki (2019), pp. 393–395.

[114] See IndustriAll Global Union (2014).

in 2014, is to ensure respect for human rights within the labour and social environment by promoting decent work throughout the supply chain. What makes this agreement exceptional is that it emphasizes the relevance of the freedom of association and the right to bargain collectively in improving labour protection within the supply chain. According to the agreement, these rights provide workers in the supply chain with mechanisms to monitor and enforce their rights at work.[115] Lately, the agreement was renewed so that a global trade union committee was set up for implementation of the agreement at global level. In addition, the agreement sets out an establishment of joint training policies and programmes that involve the workers at Inditex factories and suppliers in order to make progress on the promotion of social dialogue and workplace equality.[116]

It is well known that problems of lack of monitoring and enforcement are a central challenge for IFAs. Although some IFAs include implementation and enforcement mechanisms, sometimes these agreements are loosely formed as a complementary part of the CSR documentation of an MNE. However, connections between IFAs and CSR strategies of companies vary, and a company-specific IFA may support company CSR strategy by concretizing it in social issues and boosting its enforcement.[117] IFAs may transform the CSR policies of multinationals into more concrete and binding commitments. Many IFAs provide a complaints procedure for workers if a violation of workers' rights as stated in the agreement occurs.[118] These agreements are often based on the idea that any disputes or breaches of labour rights governed are handled in the company in cooperation with workers' representatives. However, there is evidence of problems involved with the efficiency of company-specific dispute-settlement mechanisms. This raises a concern about the extent to which such agreements can be regarded as advancing transnational accountability without further developing their implementation and enforcement. A particular problem often lies in implementing IFAs in relation to suppliers.[119] Often these agreements merely include a commitment to inform or encourage suppliers to respect the agreement or parts of it without stating the consequences of failure to do so. Moreover, although trade unions would seem to prefer monitoring compliance with IFAs by employees and trade unions themselves, related structures and resources are largely lacking.[120]

Altogether, the impact of IFAs on labour rights and protection remains limited but the potential involved cannot be overlooked. With advancing globalization and complex modes of global production, it is important that transnational agreements

---

[115] See Chacartegui (2019), pp. 547–548.

[116] See Global Framework Agreement between Industria de Diseño Textil, S.A. (Inditex, S.A.) and IndustriAll Global Union on the implementation of International Labour Standards throughout the Supply Chain of Inditex. Available at: http://www.industriall-union.org/sites/default/files/uploads/documents/GFAs/signed_gfa_inditex_-_english.pdf. Accessed 29 April 2020.

[117] See Liukkunen (2014).

[118] See Liukkunen (2019a), pp. 49–53.

[119] See Blasi and Bair (2019).

[120] See Liukkunen (2019a), p. 53.

can be drawn to cover companies' entire field of operations. They produce transnational normativities that derive from denationalised social dialogue based on particular normative-institutional development in a transnational setting. However, their efficient implementation would need further action and structural solutions at the international level.[121] The ILO could play a central role in these efforts.

7.2 *Expansion of the Transnational Construction of Labour Standards*

With privatization of labour standards-creation, several developments point to the expansion of regulatory approaches that influence labour protection and labour standards on a transnational level with a limited account of labour rights. These developments emphasize heterogeneous labour standards creation by widening number of non-state actors that claim regulatory authority. Transnational labour standards have evolved regardless of the traditional system of international labour standards, but they should be viewed against this system to evaluate their role. On the other hand, privatization development entails particular governance structures, as the Accord on Fire and Building Safety in Bangladesh from 2013 demonstrates. This agreement, designed to make safe the working environment for the Bangladeshi Ready Made Garment Industry, was made between retailers and global brands and national as well as international trade unions.[122] The Bangladesh Accord is legally binding and has a specific governance model which involves the ILO. The regulatory framework created brings together global and local strategies of labour governance and seeks to facilitate cross-border social dialogue in a novel way.

In the framing of labour governance at transnational level, foreign trade agreements (FTAs) have gained noteworthy significance and visibility in setting goals that integrate pursuit of labour protection to trade and investment. For example, the recent EU Free Trade Agreement with Vietnam includes a sustainability chapter which governs (i) recognition of the beneficial role of decent work; (ii) facilitation of trade and investment in environmental goods and services, which are relevant for climate change; (iii) development and participation in voluntary initiatives and regulatory measures to establish high-level labour and environmental protection; and (iv) promotion of corporate social responsibility. As this agreement shows, the decent work goal has gained a foothold in recent developments of FTAs but with obvious imprecision. Although labour standards have found their way into trade agreement clauses the differentiation of outcomes is remarkable and their ultimate

---

[121] See Liukkunen (2014).

[122] See the Accord on Fire and Building Safety in Bangladesh, 2013. Available at: https://admin.bangladeshaccord.org/wp-content/uploads/2018/08/2013-Accord.pdf. Accessed 29 April 2020; and the Accord on Fire and Building Safety in Bangladesh, 2018. Available at: https://admin.bangladeshaccord.org/wp-content/uploads/2018/08/2018-Accord.pdf. Accessed 29 April 2020.

goal often blurred.[123] There is also a trend of refraining from adding promotion of collective labour rights to FTAs. Generally, a vocabulary of labour standards instead of labour rights is preferred.[124]

In the transnational dimension, new kind of regulators and ways of regulating complement but also compete with regulatory approaches and contents advocated by the ILO. Moreover, they build a perspective on labour standards that leaves traditional labour rights frames in the shade. Importantly, the transnational dimension of labour protection is not only complementary to domestic and international approaches but also has its own normative setting from which it stems and evolves, fulfilling lacunas by creation of transnational normativities within labour law beyond state frontiers.

However, fundamental labour rights integration with transnational normative development poses a challenge to the ILO. In a transnational setting, social justice cannot be achieved merely through material regulation as the institutional space of regulatory power gains additional significance. Hence, more attention needs to be placed on the procedural and institutional dimensions of regulatory efforts in a transnational regulatory environment.

8 Conclusion

The process of transnationalization of labour law affects the traditional labour law paradigm with profound consequences for our understanding of the purpose and role of labour law, consequences that derive from the growing significance of transnational norm-setting in a cross-border frame. In recent decades, normative developments have occurred that detach spatial dimension of labour protection from the territorial allocation of protection as the sole starting point.[125] Despite legal ambiguity and diverse experience in different states, transnational agreements add new regulatory frameworks and mechanisms to collective labour law. They involve a new kind of enhancement of regulatory instruments developing collective rule-making capacities and a normative-institutional dimension of labour law in a cross-border setting.

In the Western portrait, labour law reflects a certain tradition and culture, and a strong influence from labour market organizations. Against this background, an assessment of the changing legal landscape of labour protection requires a contextual point of departure. However, globalization challenges this constellation and narrows its premises. Countries with a lower level of development cannot be left behind. The objective of decent work requires inclusive responses to global

---

[123] See also Banks (2011), pp. 48–49.

[124] See Brown (2015, 2016).

[125] See Mundlak (2009).

challenges of labour regulation.[126] This challenges old models of labour law thinking and initiates a search for collective participation mechanisms that best fulfil this requirement.

Demands of flexibility posed to labour law have challenged old conceptual underpinnings and shaped the understanding of objectives set to labour standards, shifting the perspective from a labour rights-based frame towards a standards-based one. However, there is a growing need to pay heed to increasing vulnerabilities in order to develop ways to make regulatory frames of labour law more inclusive. This requires a shift back to labour rights-oriented thinking. As uncertainties are growing in the labour market, states need to reactivate in ensuring a better balance between flexibility and security. Simultaneously, instead of maintaining the level of formal categorizations a deeper account is required so that all who work or would like to work are taken at sight. This scene alters the perspective as to questions of exclusion and inclusion; and it should alter labour law talk too.[127]

We have a broadening picture of the ways in which decentralization is changing domestic collective bargaining regimes—a picture that draws attention to the basic functions of collective labour law. Work for fairer globalization has met one of its hardest setbacks in the area of collective labour rights, calling for the ILO to offer a clearer vision of the road ahead. There is a need to construct ways to develop regulatory responses that highlight not only economic necessities but also equality and protection for workers so that the objectives of collective bargaining are considered in terms of employability and competitiveness as well as in terms of labour protection and inclusivity. We should also seek to recognize the impact of the regulatory changes we are witnessing at the level of embedded normativities of labour law as this would better bring into the spotlight changes in the normative-institutional dimension of labour law.

The picture of the challenges to collective labour rights is different when their role in a transnational setting is viewed. The evolution of transnational negotiations and contractual arrangements at the level of MNEs has been an important development adding a new transnational layer to industrial relations.[128] Despite uncertainties, conclusion of transnational agreements demonstrates transnational social dialogue and institutional development which contribute to promoting compliance with fundamental labour rights and international labour standards more generally. Transnational negotiations are capable of producing rights-based regulatory frames in a cross-border setting. However, core labour standards should be more firmly included in these developments. In transnational regulatory developments, much work remains to pursue the commitment to core labour standards. As the status of fundamental labour rights is particularly weak in cross-border settings, the international commitment to foster regulatory development building on these rights would

[126] See also Hepple (2005), p. 19.

[127] See for example Alan Bogg and Cynthia Estlund proposing novel ways to view and broaden the sphere of the right to the freedom of association, in Bogg and Estlund (2014).

[128] Liukkunen (2019a), p. 55.

require a renewed role for the ILO. In order to deal with vulnerabilities that escape the state law frame, the ILO decent work agenda should include a transnational dimension.

While historical explanations of the evolution of labour law in industrial societies can be built with a focus on domestic labour law models, the world of work has been so strongly affected by globalization that an isolated evaluation of individual national-level regulatory frames for labour protection has become inadequate. The risk of inequality, unemployment and poverty is an essential threat to every society, and labour standards are meant to offer a buffer against reduced protection.[129] In essence, any sketch of the labour question of our time has a global face.[130]

Importantly, the regulatory frame of sustainable development based on the key elements of the ILO decent work agenda, employment creation, social protection, rights at work, and social dialogue, should be more firmly integrated into global perspectives of the labour question if it is to work. Within this frame, a more concrete regulatory pursuit initiated by the ILO would send strong signals although it would require adopting the goal of a decent life as a frame to address situations which hinder decent work.

Still, even in fostering these pursuits, regulatory strategies that are based on decent work provide a solid point of departure only if fundamental labour rights are strengthened. Decent work connects the fight against inequality to the social dialogue and enabling the collective voice of workers. As such, it brings together the core content of the system of international labour standards and aspirations deriving from the origins of the ILO.

References

Alston P (2004) Core labour standards and the transformation of the international labour rights regime. Eur J Int Law 15(3):457–522

Alston P, Heenan J (2004) Shrinking the international labor code: an unintended consequence of the 1998 ILO Declaration on Fundamental Principles and Rights at Work. NYU J Int Law Polit 36(2&3):221–264

Araki T (2019) Japan. In: Liukkunen U (ed) Collective bargaining in labour law regimes: a global perspective. Ius Comparatum – global studies in comparative law, vol 32. Springer, Cham

Awad AB (2005) Decent work as a national goal: the experience of the Decent Work Pilot Programme (DWPP) and other related initiatives, 2nd South-East Asia and the Pacific Subregional Tripartite Forum on Decent Work, Melbourne, Australia, 2005

[129] The Philadelphia Declaration of 1944 states that poverty anywhere constitutes a danger to prosperity everywhere and that the war against want must be fought as an international effort where representatives of workers and employers are equal participants along with government representatives.

[130] The renewed universal approach of the ILO is manifested, for example, in the most recent Convention concerning the Elimination of Violence and Harassment in the World of Work (No. 190) adopted on 21 June 2019, which governs all workers regardless of the form of employment. See Article 2 of the Convention.

Banks K (2011) Trade, labor and international governance: an inquiry into the potential effectiveness of the new international labor law. Berkeley J Emp & Lab L 32(1):45–142
Blasi J, Bair J (2019) An analysis of multiparty bargaining models for global supply chains. ILO conditions of work and employment, report series no. 105. International Labour Office, Geneva
Bogg A (2015) Labour law and the trade unions: autonomy and betrayal. In: Bogg A, Costello C, Davies ACL, Adams-Prassl J (eds) The autonomy of labour law. Hart, Oxford
Bogg A, Estlund C (2014) Freedom of association and the right to contest: getting back to basics. In: Bogg A, Novitz T (eds) Voices at work: continuity and change in the common law world. Oxford University Press, Oxford
Bogg A, Costello C, Davies ACL, Adams-Prassl J (2015) Introduction: exploring autonomy. In: Bogg A, Costello C, Davies ACL, Adams-Prassl J (eds) The autonomy of labour law. Hart, Oxford
Brown RC (2015) Asian and US perspectives on labor rights under international trade agreements compared. In: Marx A, Wouters J, Rayp G, Beke L (eds) Global governance of labour rights: assessing the effectiveness of transnational public and private policy initiatives. Edward Elgar, Cheltenham
Brown RC (2016) China – U.S. implementation of ILO standards by BITs and pieces (FTAs). In: Liukkunen U, Chen Y (eds) Fundamental labour rights in China – legal implementation and cultural logic. Springer, Cham
Carr M, Chen M (2004) Globalization, social exclusion and work: with special reference to informal employment and gender, Working paper no. 20. International Labour Office, Geneva
Chacartegui C (2019) Spain. In: Liukkunen U (ed) Collective bargaining in labour law regimes: a global perspective. Ius Comparatum – global studies in comparative law, vol 32. Springer, Cham
Chen Y, Liukkunen U (2019) Enclave governance and transnational labour law – a case study of Chinese workers on strike in Africa. Nordic J Int Law 88(4):558–586
Collins H (2015) Contractual autonomy. In: Bogg A, Costello C, Davies ACL, Adams-Prassl J (eds) The autonomy of labour law. Hart, Oxford
Costello C, Freedland M (eds) (2014) Migrants at work: immigration and vulnerability in labour law. Oxford University Press, Oxford
Danielsen D (2005) How corporations govern: taking corporate power seriously in transnational regulation and governance. Harv Int Law J 46(2):411–426
Davidov G (2002) The three axes of employment relationships: a characterization of workers in need of protection. Univ Toronto Law J 52(4):357–418
Davies P, Freedland M (1983) Kahn-Freund's labour and the law, 3rd edn. Stevens & Sons, London
Daza JL (2005) Informal economy, undeclared work and labour administration. International Labour Office, Geneva
Doorey DJ (2015) A transnational law of just transitions for climate change and labour. In: Blackett A, Trebilcock A (eds) Research handbook on transnational labour law. Edward Elgar, Cheltenham
Doorey DJ (2017) Just transitions law: putting labour law to work on climate change. JELP 30(2):201–239
Dukes R (2014) The labour constitution: the enduring idea of labour law. Oxford University Press, Oxford
Estlund C (2015) Working together transnationally. In: Blackett A, Trebilcock A (eds) Research handbook on transnational labour law. Edward Elgar, Cheltenham
Fields GS (2003) International labour standards and decent work: perspectives from the developing world. In: Flanagan RJ, Gould WB IV (eds) International labor standards: globalization, trade and public policy. Stanford University Press, Stanford
Frey DF, MacNaughton G (2016) A human rights lens on full employment and decent work in the 2030 sustainable development agenda. J Workplace Rights:1–13
Hepple B (2002) Enforcement: the law and politics of cooperation and compliance. In: Hepple B (ed) Social and labour rights in a global context. International and comparative perspectives. Cambridge University Press, Cambridge

Hepple B (2005) Labour laws and global trade. Hart, Oxford
Human Rights Council (2011) Report of the Special Representative of the Secretary General on the issue of human rights and transnational corporations and other business enterprises, John Ruggie. Guiding Principles on Business and Human Rights: implementing the United Nations 'protect, respect and remedy' framework
ILO (1999a) Report of the Director-General: Decent work, International Labour Conference, 87th Session, Geneva, 1999. International Labour Office, Geneva
ILO (1999b) Decent work for all in a global economy: an ILO perspective. Submission by Juan Somavia, Director-General, International Labour Office, to the Third WTO Ministerial Conference, Seattle, 1999
ILO (2001) Report of the Director-General: Reducing the decent work deficit – a global challenge, International Labour Conference, 89th Session, Geneva, 2001. International Labour Office, Geneva
ILO (2002a) Decent work and the informal economy, International Labour Conference, 90th Session, Geneva, 2002. International Labour Office, Geneva
ILO (2002b) Health and safety at work: a trade union priority. Labour Education 2002/1, No. 126
ILO (2004) A fair globalization. The role of the ILO. Report of the Director-General on the World Commission on the Social Dimension of Globalization, International Labour Conference, 92nd Session, Geneva, 2004. International Labour Office, Geneva
ILO (2015) Guidelines for a just transition towards environmentally sustainable economies and societies for all. International Labour Office, Geneva
ILO (2017) Global estimates of modern slavery: forced labour and forced marriage. International Labour Office, Geneva
ILO (2018) Women and men in the informal economy: a statistical picture, 3rd edn. International Labour Office, Geneva
ILO (2020) Promoting employment and decent work in a changing landscape. Report of the Committee of Experts on the Application of Conventions and Recommendations (articles 19, 22 and 35 of the Constitution) Report III (Part B). International Labour Conference, 109th Session, Geneva, 2020. International Labour Office, Geneva
ILO (n.d.-a) Ratifications of fundamental Conventions by country. Available at: https://www.ilo.org/dyn/normlex/en/f?p=1000:10011:1143555406784::::P10011_DISPLAY_BY:1. Accessed 29 Apr 2020
ILO (n.d.-b) Decent Work Pilot Programme – DWPP. Available at: https://www.ilo.org/public/english/bureau/dwpp/. Accessed 29 Apr 2020
ILO Committee of Experts (2010) General Report and observations concerning particular countries, Report III (Part 1A). International Labour Conference, 99th Session, Geneva, 2010. International Labour Office, Geneva
ILO Committee of Freedom of Association (2012) Report in which the committee requests to be kept informed of development - Report No 365. Case No 2820 (Greece) - Complaint date: 21 October 2010. Available at: https://www.ilo.org/dyn/normlex/en/f?p=1000:50002:0::NO:50002:P50002_COMPLAINT_TEXT_ID:3087085. Accessed 29 Apr 2020
ILO, OECD, IOM, UNICEF (2019) Ending child labour, forced labour and human trafficking in global supply chains. Alliance 8.7 Action Group on Supply Chains, Geneva
IndustriAll Global Union (2014) Inditex. Available at: http://www.industriall-union.org/inditex. Accessed 29 Apr 2020
Intergovernmental Working Group on a Code of Conduct (1982) Report of the Intergovernmental Working Group on a Code of Conduct on its fifteenth, sixteenth and seventeenth sessions, UN Commission on Transnational Corporations, 8th Session, Manila, 1982
Javillier JC (2003) Introduction. In: ILO, Fundamental rights at work and international labour standards. International Labour Office, Geneva
Kun A (2019) Hungary. In: Liukkunen U (ed) Collective bargaining in labour law regimes: a global perspective. Ius Comparatum – global studies in comparative law, vol 32. Springer, Cham

Langille B (2018) Human development: a way out of labour law's fly bottle. In: Collins H, Lester G, Mantouvalou V (eds) Philosophical foundations of labour law. Oxford University Press, Oxford
Langille B (2019a) The political economy of decency. In: Politakis GP, Kohiyama T, Lieby T (eds) ILO100 – law for social justice. International Labour Office, Geneva
Langille B (ed) (2019b) The capability approach to labour law. Oxford University Press, Oxford
Leary VA (1997) The WTO and the social clause: post-Singapore. Eur J Intl Law 8(1):118–122
Liukkunen U (2005) Globalisaatio, EU ja henkilöstön osallistuminen [Globalization, the EU and employee participation]. Edita, Helsinki
Liukkunen U (2013) Yritystoiminnan muutokset ja yhteistoiminta. Tutkimus kansallisesta ja transnationaalista työoikeudesta [Corporate restructuring and participation. A study of national and transnational labour law]. Forum iuris. Helsingin yliopisto, oikeustieteellinen tiedekunta, Helsinki
Liukkunen U (2014) Transnational labour law and fundamental labour rights: making Chinese workers matter? In: Liukkunen U, Chen Y (eds) China and ILO fundamental principles and rights at work. Bulletin of Comparative Labour Relations, No. 86. Kluwer Law International, Alphen aan den Rijn
Liukkunen U (2016) ILO and child labour regulation in China: prospects and complexities. In: Liukkunen U, Chen Y (eds) Fundamental labour rights in China – legal implementation and cultural logic. Springer, Cham
Liukkunen U (2019a) The role of collective bargaining in labour law regimes: a global approach. In: Liukkunen U (ed) Collective bargaining in labour law regimes: a global perspective. Ius Comparatum – global studies in comparative law, vol 32. Springer, Cham
Liukkunen U (ed) (2019b) Collective bargaining in labour law regimes: a global perspective. Ius Comparatum – global studies in comparative law, vol 32. Springer, Cham
Liukkunen U, Chen Y (2016) Developing fundamental labour rights in China: a new approach to implementation. In: Liukkunen U, Chen Y (eds) Fundamental labour rights in China – legal implementation and cultural logic. Springer, Cham
MacNaughton G, Frey DF (2011) Decent work for all: a holistic human rights approach. Am Univ Int Law Rev 26(2):441–484
Magnani M (2019) Italy. In: Liukkunen U (ed) Collective bargaining in labour law regimes: a global perspective. Ius Comparatum – global studies in comparative law, vol 32. Springer, Cham
Maia DCM (2019) Brazil. In: Liukkunen U (ed) Collective bargaining in labour law regimes: a global perspective. Ius Comparatum – global studies in comparative law, vol 32. Springer, Cham
Marx A, Soares J, van Acker W (2015) The protection of international labour rights: a longitudinal analysis of the protection of the rights of freedom of association and collective bargaining over 30 years in 73 countries. In: Marx A, Wouters J, Rayp G, Beke L (eds) Global governance of labour rights: assessing the effectiveness of transnational public and private policy initiatives. Edward Elgar, Cheltenham
Maupain F (2013) The future of the International Labour Organization in the global economy. Hart, Oxford
Mazuyer E (2019) France. In: Liukkunen U (ed) Collective bargaining in labour law regimes: a global perspective. Ius Comparatum – global studies in comparative law, vol 32. Springer, Cham
Moreau MA (2013) The reconceptualization of the employment relationship and labor rights through transnationality. Comp Lab Law & Policy J 34(3):697–714
Müller T, Platzer HW, Rüb S (2008) International Framework Agreements – Opportunities and Limitations of a New Tool of Global Trade Union Policy. Briefing Papers No. 8/2008
Mundlak G (2009) De-territorializing labor law. Law & Ethics Human Rights 3(2):189–222
Papadakis K, Casale G, Tsotroudi K (2008) International framework agreements as elements of a cross-border industrial relations framework. In: Papadakis K (ed) Cross-border social dialogue and agreements: an emerging global industrial relations framework? International Institute of Labour Studies, Geneva
Scelle G (1930) L'Organisation Internationale du Travail et le B.I.T. M. Rivière, Paris

Seifert A (2014) European economic governance and the labor laws of the E. U. Member States. Comp Lab Law & Policy J 35(3):311–330

Supiot A (2012) The spirit of Philadelphia: social justice vs. the total market. Verso, London

Tuori K (2016) Ratio and Voluntas: the tension between reason and will in law. Ashgate, Farnham

UN (n.d.) SDG 8: Decent Work and Economic Growth. Available at: https://www.un.org/sustainabledevelopment/economic-growth/. Accessed 29 Apr 2020

Waas B (2020) How to improve monitoring and enforcement of international labour standards? In: Halonen T, Liukkunen U (eds) International Labour Organization and global social governance. Springer, Cham

Weiss M (2013) International labour standards: a complex public-private policy mix. Int J Comp Lab Law & Indus Rel 29(1):7–20

Weitz N, Carlsen H, Skånberg K, Dzebo A, Viaud V (2019) SDGs and the environment in the EU: a systems view to improve coherence. Project report. Stockholm Environment Institute. Available at: https://www.sei.org/publications/sdg-synergies-environment-eu/. Accessed 29 Apr 2020

Wolff J (2018) Structures of exploitation. In: Collins H, Lester G, Mantouvalou V (eds) Philosophical foundations of labour law. Oxford University Press, Oxford

World Commission on the Social Dimension of Globalization (2004) A fair globalization: creating opportunities for all. International Labour Office, Geneva. Available at: https://www.ilo.org/public/english/wcsdg/docs/report.pdf. Accessed 29 Apr 2020

Ulla Liukkunen is Professor of Labour Law and Private International Law at the University of Helsinki. She is also the Director of the Finnish Center of Chinese Law and Chinese Legal Culture and a Member of the Board of the European China Law Studies Association. Professor Liukkunen has published widely on labour law, private international law, comparative law, transnational law and governance of the social dimension of globalization. She has led two Academy of Finland international labour law research projects, "ILO Core Labour Standards Implementation in China: Legal Architecture and Cultural Logic" and "Employee Participation and Collective Bargaining in the Era of Globalization – Nordic and Chinese Perspectives" and acted as a senior researcher in the Academy of Finland Centre of Excellence "Foundations of European Law and Polity". Professor Liukkunen has broad experience in national and EU law drafting as a Counsellor in Legislative Affairs of the Ministry of Labour. She has acted as an expert and chair in several international projects on labour law and private international law.

What Happened to International Labour Standards and Human Rights at Work?

Kari Tapiola

Contents

K. Tapiola (✉)
International Labour Organization, Geneva, Switzerland
e-mail: tapiola@ilo.org

T. Halonen, U. Liukkunen (eds.), *International Labour Organization and Global Social Governance*, https://doi.org/10.1007/978-3-030-55400-2_3

1 Introduction

There has been debate on the international labour standards of the ILO for the whole hundred years of its existence. This has concerned the choice of topics themselves, the detail in which the norms have been set out, and their ratification and subsequent application and supervision. During the last 40 years the debate has been moving from one extreme to another. The post-World War II consensus on the need to maintain a balance between economic and social progress was an element in reconstruction and of industrialized countries' growth and welfare. As of the 1980s, this consensus broke down. With increased emphasis on market forces, labour standards started being seen as rigidities and impediments to growth. Once the Cold War ended, a question in the early 1990s was posed in almost brutal terms: now that the common enemy—communist state power—was gone, was there still a need for the ILO and its standards?

Socialist political and economic structures crumbled as of 1989 at a pace no one had foreseen. This in turn brought about a new transparency and a new openness of the entire world economy, enabled by technological change and the utilization of real-time sourcing and production. However, the good news of the spread of democracy and markets was accompanied by a shock when especially Western consumers found out that new and affordable products from emerging countries were—or could be—produced by very young children in miserable conditions. Consumers reacted for moral reasons; workers reacted because cheap imports affected their jobs. All of a sudden there was a call for universal rules on labour again. After having first been sidelined in the frenzy of transition, fundamental rights at work became a hotly contested issue in globalization and international trade.

As the world trading system was being reorganized, the question of fundamental rights at work turned around the call for a "social clause", which was designed to make access to world trade conditional on observance of labour rights. The world trade lobby succeeded in keeping the issue away from the World Trade Organization, which was set up in 1995. Efforts to keep the issue alive were largely confined to the ILO, which remained, as before, the custodian of international labour standards.

The contents of fundamental human rights at work were clarified by the ILO in the Declaration on Fundamental Principles and Rights at Work, adopted in 1998.[1] The follow-up to the Declaration boosted these standards by promising technical cooperation, with which they now became increasingly linked. The ILO introduced an extensive programme of assistance to developing countries for freedom of association, the right to collective bargaining, freedom from forced and child labour and multiform action against all forms of discrimination at work.

These fundamental rights—or "core labour standards" as they were also called—were universally accepted as an element of the new globalized world order. Support for applying them and even pressure to do so was assisted by extra-budgetary

[1] ILO, Declaration on Fundamental Principles and Rights at Work. Adopted by the International Labour Conference, 86th Session, Geneva, 18 June 1998 (Annex revised 15 June 2010).

resources from the industrialized countries. For many of them, this was the second best option once trade sanctions were discouraged. Fundamental rights made their way into international documents governing trade, investment and cooperation. They were seen to translate the social dimensions of the new world economy, while promoting them was akin to the role of the ILO after the two World Wars.

To what extent this new focus on social justice was genuine or simply words, or opportunism, is anybody's guess. Yet the formula of ILO technical cooperation for a level playing field for trade and a means of raising standards among the emerging participants of the trading system was appealing. Soon over half of the technical cooperation of the ILO was in the field of fundamental rights at work, most of it aimed at eliminating child labour.[2]

Since the financial crisis, which burst out in 2008, and since the recent worldwide political slide towards extremism, nationalism, xenophobia and brutal egoism, we have again heard less about rights at work.

However, the spell of neo-brutalism that we are living through springs from the same source as the desire for social and labour rules. Both are driven by fear that the forces of globalization have become an existential threat to individuals and societies. These concerns arise from uncertainties about employment, incomes and maintenance of social status in an increasingly volatile world. Two images illustrate what has happened. Products from subcontractors with workers in shabby conditions in underdeveloped societies have been flooding the markets. Especially since 2015, a highly visible flow of migrants and refugees across borders has also been occurring.

These images have been destabilizing industrialized countries while at the same time allowing a glimpse of the hopes and despairs of the developing world. Both workers and entrepreneurs in all countries have been affected. Most vulnerable have been the categories accounting for a significant amount of employment: the self-employed and micro- and small and medium enterprises. At the same time, while the line dividing opportunity and exclusion has remained endemic in less fortunate countries, it has also cut through the richest societies of the world.

The question of fundamental principles and rights at work is an issue for each and every society, especially taking into account modern slavery and trafficking, zero hours employment contracts, "Uberization" of urban services, the platform and gig economies and profiling due to political suspicions, as well as harassment and violence at work. Our new divisions are between the wealthy and fortunate on the one hand and the struggling and excluded on the other hand at all points of the compass. One dividing factor remains the way and extent to which labour standards are applied. In this complex situation the linkages between standards designed as fundamental and other—more "technical"—standards are even more topical than in earlier times. In a nutshell, these are so interlinked that it is not possible to have any one without the others—as I shall aim to demonstrate in this chapter.

[2] Tapiola (2018).

2 Development of International Labour Standards

International labour law was a novel notion in 1919. The standards adopted by the ILO are derived from the labour principles of its Constitution.[3] These principles had in turn been formulated by the trade unions during the First World War and were originally proposed as the "labour clauses" of the Peace Treaty. The Versailles Treaty did not produce a lasting peace or universal happiness, but at least the system of rights expressed in international labour standards was born.

The labour principles of 1919 are the basis of the International Labour Code. These principles cover a broad scope of labour rights, starting with freedom of association, hours of work, employment policy, maternity protection, labour inspection, social security provisions, minimum age for employment and the health and safety of different categories of workers. Most of the labour legislation and practice in the world today has been shaped by these principles.

For many decades the corpus of international labour standards grew at a regular pace. Most issues were treated by either a Convention or a Recommendation, or in a few cases a Protocol. Conventions become binding through national ratification; Recommendations form an integral part of the standards system and although they are not binding, in principle they should apply to everyone. Other instruments, such as Declarations and codes of practice, have complemented the ILO toolkit. They do not have the status of labour standards, but they do give guidance for treating labour and social issues at national level, including by labour legislation. From the outset, this system has been a combination of what we occasionally call "hard" and "soft" law.

3 Human Rights Standards

After the Second World War, the normative foundation of the ILO was aligned with the need to reaffirm democratic rights and promote development. What we know as fundamental rights at work were created by standard-setting on human rights after the 1944 International Labour Conference in Philadelphia. This coincided with the early years of the United Nations, democratization, decolonization and the Cold War.

Discrimination and forced labour had come into a new focus during the labour and extermination camps of the Second Word War. As decolonization proceeded, the heavy weight of discrimination and of imperial-age economic interests continued to hamper the achievement of true national sovereignty.

Decolonization created the African group in the United Nations and the ILO. When racial segregation not only continued but became increasingly brutal in South and Southern Africa, the issue of discrimination rose to the top of the agenda. South Africa was forced to withdraw from the ILO in 1964, but apartheid remained

[3] Article 427, Section II, Chapter VI, Part XIII of the Treaty of Peace of Versailles 1919.

prominently on the agenda through special procedures in which trade unions and employers participated. At the same time, the United States had to accept significant measures for desegregation in its Southern States.

The shattering war-time experiences of racial discrimination, forced labour and denial of rights of not only workers but also employers played an important role in building a consensus on human rights at work. Employers had still been ambivalent about the role of Mussolini's fascist corporations in Italy, but subsequently the course of the war showed that their organizations could be equally threatened by totalitarian régimes. In 1919, the language of the labour principles of the Constitution had affirmed that freedom of association was a right of workers and employers alike.[4] In the early Cold War years, the ILO recognized that the independence of employers was also covered by the concept of trade union rights.[5]

The questions of freedom of association and forced labour found new relevance because of the practice of communist countries. What had been a reaction to the atrocities of the fascist regimes carried over to discussion on social, individual and economic liberties in reconstruction and economic development. In the labour field, during the Cold War, certain human rights—above all freedom of association—defined the side on which you were between the market economy and communism. This placed the main part of the trade unions on the same side of the divide as employers. In practice this determined much of the standard-setting after 1948 well beyond the fundamental principles and rights at work. Multiple compromises were called for in the period between 1945 and 1989—between employers and workers, between industrialized and developing countries, and between radical and moderate elements of—especially—the Workers' Group.

During the long tenure of David Morse as Director-General (1948–1970), the ILO stressed employment, skills and social policies which were guided by the tripartite engagement at the national level of governments, employers and trade unions.[6] Significant normative work was done on labour inspection and administration, social security, occupational safety and health, employment and labour market policies, gender equality, paid educational leave and holidays with pay.

These were the building blocks of a liberal social development model, based on a negotiated balance of interests between and within different constituent groups of the ILO. Fifty years ago it earned the ILO the Nobel Peace Prize.

Soon thereafter, however, global changes and technological innovation conspired to change the parameters. Multinational enterprises moved production across national borders and, in extreme cases, could cause political upheavals, such as the coup d'état against Salvador Allende in Chile in 1973. Oil crises and debt crises started shaking expectations of stability and continuous growth and prosperity.

---

[4] Ibid.

[5] ILO, Resolution concerning the Protection of Trade Union Rights. Adopted by the International Labour Conference, 38th Session, Geneva, 1–23 June 1955.

[6] Morse (1969), pp. 57–59.

The result was a relatively rapid sea-change. One of the reasons for this was the realization that in large parts of the world trying to reproduce the industrialized countries' development model did not lead to sustained employment. In the 1980s, with—especially—European growth lagging, calls for giving more freedom to market forces were accompanied by new technology, which allowed real-time cross-border production and severed many physical employer-employee links. This was followed by accelerated liberalization of trade and capital movements.

4 Establishing the Social Dimension

In the new situation after the end of the Cold War and the global opening of markets, the Declaration on Fundamental Principles and Rights at Work of 1998 and its follow-up activities expressed an underlying aim of the ILO: to strengthen the social dimension of international economic and social policies. After the First World War, the founding of the ILO had brought a social dimension to peacemaking. After the Second World War, the ILO had provided the social dimension of both reconstruction and—once decolonization got under way—of development. The Cold War ended without a political or social peace deal with "labour clauses". The notion of universal fundamental rights at work had to assume much of the role of providing for a social dimension. In the debate on standards versus deregulation in the global market, it worked as a smart battle ram, piercing resistance to all kinds of standards. But it could not serve as a broad social contract.

The 1998 Declaration contained consensus on a short-list of "fundamental" social and labour rights: freedom of association, the right to collective bargaining, abolition of forced labour, elimination of child labour and rejection of discrimination in employment and occupation, including equal pay for work of equal value between women and men.

Each of these four categories of rights was linked to a Convention. Three of the four categories had Conventions which at least in principle were universally acceptable: Nos 87/98 on freedom of association and collective bargaining, Nos 29/105 on forced labour and Nos 100/111 on discrimination and equal remuneration. Child labour was attached to this short list a bit later.

The years when David Morse, Wilfred Jenks and Francis Blanchard led the ILO saw discussion on trade and labour standards. The debate did not in any way start only in the 1990s. Additionally, both recognized that besides human rights at work such issues as a living wage, labour inspection, health and safety and basic social security should be addressed. These were all derived from the original Constitution of the ILO but the Conventions on them did not enjoy the same status and consensus as the human rights Conventions.

In the early 1990s it was politically necessary to have a manageable list of standards because of the de facto link to international trade. The OECD produced a study which showed how difficult it could be to deal with an extended list of up to ten categories of standards, in particular if the link to trade would mean intensified enforcement measures through existing or new supervisory mechanisms of Conventions.[7]

Conventions on wages, social security or occupational safety and health were not as widely ratified, and even the leading ones covered only parts of the strategic decent work objectives to which they belonged. A large number of Conventions, which all had several technical provisions, could thus have become new arguments in trade policies. As the stated aim of the post-Cold War debate was liberalization of international trade, new entrants to the markets feared that raising too many social issues could negate their advantages. The four "fundamentals" were known and reasonably safe. A linkage with social security provisions, occupational safety and health or the need to ensure a living wage would have been one bridge too far.

Making an operative link to trade through any kind of sanctions mechanism was anathema both for emerging countries and employers. However, promoting the ratification and application of fundamental Conventions was not. The four categories had been established at the United Nations Social Summit in Copenhagen in 1995, with heavy involvement by ILO constituents. The Conventions on freedom of association, collective bargaining, child and forced labour and discrimination were formally recognized as human rights. All countries which had ratified them should fully respect their legal obligations while all others should do their best to live up to their principles.[8]

After Copenhagen, ILO Director-General Michel Hansenne launched a ratification campaign on the relevant Conventions. At that moment the Minimum Age Convention No. 138 was quietly added to the list of "core" Conventions as the then applicable standard on child labour.

At the same time, a need clearly existed for an additional human rights standard on child labour. The earliest labour legislation at the beginning of the nineteenth Century had been on child labour. In the ILO, child labour had always been treated through Conventions on the minimum age for employment. This reflected the fact that the age of moving into full-time employment should permit compulsory education, particularly after universal schooling had become the norm towards the end of the nineteenth Century. Sectoral Conventions adopted by the ILO were in 1973 taken over by the Minimum Age Convention No. 138. However, the ratification rate of this Convention was meagre, and it had not been recognized as a priority Convention subject to more intense scrutiny.

When the need for benchmarks to define what was most intolerable in the work of children came up, the Minimum Age Convention was found to contain a useable formula establishing age limits as well as flexibility linked to levels of national development and the nature of work. When in 1999 a new Convention on the Worst Forms of Child Labour No. 182 was adopted, it built upon this Convention instead of revising it. The ratification rate of the Worst Forms of Child Labour Convention

---

[7] OECD (1996).

[8] UN (1995), para 54 (b).

has broken all records, also delivering ratifications of the Minimum Age Convention at a rate which had been unthinkable before.

Child labour was included in the four categories of fundamental rights because of the emotionally strong effect of finding out that child labour was a factor in trade. It was possible to argue that while it was a normative issue, its eradication called for time-bound technical assistance programmes. It was also the item which had the lowest level of political resistance: no régime was really threatened by its elimination. Even the Gulf States agreed to remove young children from camel jockeying in widely popular competitions, sometimes replacing them with robots.

The 1998 Declaration was also supposed to offer an easier way than ratification for countries to express their commitment. Countries could report annually to the Governing Body on their efforts to realize the principles of the Conventions, and they could signal the kind of technical cooperation they felt would be necessary to support these efforts. This innovative method could be seen as positive encouragement instead of reporting on ratified Conventions, which tended to be more investigative and often controversial.

Sometimes what happens is the unexpected. The new innovative and—presumably customer-friendly—reporting mechanism was in practice soon overtaken by what could be called an escape into the safety of the established mechanism. In short, instead of availing themselves of the new and apparently "softer" opportunity, a large number of countries preferred to ratify the fundamental Conventions instead. This was a case of preferring the devil you know to the devil you don't. As a result, the overall ratification rates of the eight fundamental Conventions shot up to over 90%, with child and forced labour reaching nearly universal levels.

5 The Effects of Technical Cooperation

Such a change in the attitude to ratifications would not have been possible without increased linkage to technical cooperation. The traditional view had been that ratification of a Convention would take place only after national law and practice had been made to conform to its requirements. When technical cooperation became a recognized part of this process, and was increasingly recommended by the standards supervisory mechanism, it became acceptable to ratify at an earlier stage once the political will was there. Technical cooperation would then ensure implementation. Financing was available, as the industrialized donor countries responded rather generously to what they saw as a positive link created between trade and labour standards.

What actually happened was that in many cases, instead of countries sliding into a conflict and economic and trade sanctions, deficiencies in labour standards led to agreements on technical cooperation; this in turn provided a compelling argument against sanctions. The credibility of such arrangements was seen to be guaranteed by the fact that reporting to, and discussion by, the standards supervisory bodies of the ILO would soon reveal how sincere the engagement of the country concerned was.

Since the early 2000s, fundamental principles and rights at work have become a part of a global *aquis*. Today it is almost unthinkable that, for instance, any politician or scholar could defend child labour by referring to cultural differences or even economic necessity. Likewise, a world-wide consensus has developed on the need to take action against human trafficking, which is one of the modern-day features of forced labour.

Despite the misgivings of the emerging world, labour standards as seen through the prism of the 1998 Declaration have found their way to trade legislation as well. This has not taken place so much through outright conditionality as through trade preferences accorded to countries which desire to respect fundamental labour standards. The European trade systems opted to use the ILO's short-list for trade preferences. Most bilateral or regional free trade treaties have followed the same pattern, either referring to the fundamental Conventions or the 1998 Declaration. The United States, however, has continued to apply a broader set of criteria than the fundamentals to its trade policies. This included labour inspection. When the US trade unions filed a trade petition because an ultraliberal 2006 Georgian Labour Code—later amended—violated freedom of association principles, the case was mainly about labour inspection which the Georgian reformers of the former communist system had scrapped.[9]

What I am arguing here is that the focus on fundamental rights at work safeguarded the role of international labour standards in general. The standards and their application were seen as a remedy to the problems of globalization and not as a complication or rigidity. In addition, the wave of ratifications of the fundamental Conventions led many countries to review their position on ILO Conventions in general. The factual blockage on new ratifications of all Conventions, which characterized especially the 1980s and 1990s, is no longer there.

6 Beyond Fundamental Rights

If we assume that, by now, the case has again been made for standards, it should also be possible to expand the scope beyond fundamental rights. This does not mean going away from them, but rather beyond them. Actually, this needs to be done even for the sake of the fundamentals themselves. Their implementation needs to reach out to the full scale of decent work. Whether in the informal or the formal economy, anywhere we want to go with the fundamentals, we quickly arrive at the whole normative basis of society.

We are facing a situation which may at first appear to be contradictory. Frustration with detailed regulation, and the obligations of ratifying states compared with a

[9] Office of the United States Trade Representative (2019).

large number of non-ratifying competitors, had led to a desire to simplify the basic rules of the game around a short-list of fundamental standards. This was by and large successful. It saved the credibility of the standards system of the ILO, not least due to assistance for countries which chose to admit that the problems they experienced in applying standards were due to insufficient capacity and not inadequate political will.

However, assistance also showed that when you start to implement fundamental rights, you are faced with a large number of practical situations and have to venture into a field which is covered with other regulations and practices. To give a simple example: after 1998 some millions of US dollars were made available for freedom of association in Indonesia. One key tool of the ILO is the Committee on Freedom of Association of the Governing Body, but you do not spend millions on advising how to write complaints to the CFA. The outcome was a broad programme of social dialogue, which included support for the development of trade unions and employers' organizations.

7 A Linkage to Adam Smith

It is instructive to note that both the case for workers' right to organize and linkages between fundamental and other rights were outlined in 1776 by Adam Smith in his *The Wealth of Nations*. Smith was the prophet of liberal economics and free trade to the extent that British Prime Minister Margaret Thatcher reportedly carried his book in her voluminous handbag. Writing about the wages of labour, Adam Smith observed that workers wanted to gain as much as possible in wages while employers conceded as little as possible. Both had an interest in combining (organizing) but Parliament had prohibited the workers from doing so. The masters in turn could always collude—and tacitly did so—to keep the price of labour down.[10]

If workers were bereft of their wages, their existence could become untenable in a matter of days while employers could weather long periods of conflict. Workers could act with the "folly and extravagance of desperate men who must either starve or frighten their masters into an immediate compliance with their demands".[11] As a result, employers would call upon local authorities who would impose a settlement far short of workers' claims.

But Adam Smith went further. After having described the industrial discipline of the day, he also noted that there was a certain point below which wages could not be brought down. Workers had to earn enough to bring up a family, which might be at least twice the minimum needed for survival. What else is this than a link between organizing rights and a "living wage"?

---

[10] Smith (2012), p. 71.

[11] Ibid., p. 72.

8 A History of Linkages

In the early twentieth Century throughout Europe, the demand for an eight hour day was closely associated with the call for universal suffrage. Freedom to express a political view is an inalienable part of freedom of association. Another fundamental trade union demand was the right of workers to voluntary migration while securing equal treatment, i.e. non-discrimination, with national workers.

Factory safety has an intimate link with freedom of association. It is logical that workers are engaged through health and safety committees but also ensuring that special safety representatives, elected by the workers, have enough authority to intervene in a dangerous situation. This is one area where a look at history reminds us how much work remains to be done.

In 1911, a fire in New York City killed 146 workers, mainly young immigrant women, in the Triangle Shirtwaist Factory. Locked doors and lack of safety measures contributed to the high toll. The tragedy led soon thereafter to the adoption of factory legislation in New York. But it also had another consequence: it intensified organizing activities by the Ladies International Garment Workers' Union, a prominent American trade union. This showed that labour inspection, one of the original priorities of the ILO, is only one part of the solution. Empowering workers to defend their interests is another, and the most direct road to that is through agreements and bargaining between employers and duly authorized workers' representatives.

Fast forward to our days: we continue to experience similar factory fires and disasters in South Asia. This culminated with the collapse in 2013 of the Rana Plaza factory building in Dhaka, Bangladesh, with a death toll of 1134. International accords for compensation and increased factory safety have since been concluded in Bangladesh,[12] but there has been little progress in the fundamental question of not only hindering but assisting union organization. Also, as with the Triangle Shirtwaist Factory fire, factory owners have rarely if at all been made to answer for their responsibilities.

9 Taking a "First-Things-First" Approach

As noted above, for the ILO the main way of diminishing the use of child labour lay in applying standards on the minimum age for employment. When the opening up of global markets made child labour a priority, this standard was seen not to address with sufficient vigour the fact that large numbers of working children were well under any established minimum age, in conditions preventing education and harmful to their health and morals.

[12] Accord on Fire and Building Safety in Bangladesh, 2013. Available at: https://admin.bangladeshaccord.org/wp-content/uploads/2018/08/2013-Accord.pdf. Accessed 4 May 2020.

A "first-things-first" approach[13] was applied to legally prohibited and hazardous child labour by the Worst Forms of Child Labour Convention No. 182, which at the time of writing is only one short of ratification by all ILO member States. While the abolition of all child labour has remained the target, urgent action was to be taken against its worst forms. This time a degree of flexibility was accorded by the traditional provision that governments—together with the social partners—should determine what kind of work was hazardous and thus eliminated as a priority.

Addressing particularly urgent issues has characterized the standard setting of the ILO in the era of globalization. The ILO has increasingly focused on vulnerable groups and urgencies with such instruments as the HIV/AIDS Recommendation in 2000 and the Conventions on Domestic Workers in 2010 and Violence at Work 2019. The Protocol against trafficking, attached in 2014 to the Forced Labour Convention No. 29, belongs to this same category.

Different areas of social policy were extensively set out by Convention No. 102 of 1952, which despite wide policy agreement has gained only a limited number of ratifications. In line with the "first-things-first" approach, a normative move towards universal social security coverage was undertaken by the adoption of a Recommendation on Social Protection Floors, 2012 (No. 202). While it is not possible to globally determine minimum protection levels that could be applicable to all, the Recommendation set out the principle that everyone in every country should have at least a basic level of protection. The Recommendation does not undermine or set aside the comprehensive Social Security Convention No. 102, which remains a state of the art instrument. Nor does it aim to set minimum levels which, if enforced as the minimum everywhere, would inevitably put more pressure on those who already have achieved higher levels of protection.

At the same time the coverage of standards has extended to the informal economy with a Recommendation adopted in 2015. The Recommendation aims to increase the organizing of all workers and economic units—enterprises and households—in the entire informal economy where 62% of the global workforce is to be found. Of particular importance, too, is the Decent Work for Peace and Resilience Recommendation, 2017 (No. 205). This replaced a Recommendation adopted by the International Labour Conference in 1944 on transition from war to peace. The Recommendation outlines measures for relief and reconstruction after not only war and conflict but also natural disasters. The employment and social effects of the COVID-19 pandemic have made this Recommendation particularly topical.

In the area of maritime labour, all existing instruments—binding and nonbinding—were in 2006 combined in a coherent, living and continuously updated instrument for an inherently globalized sector of work. It incorporates both obligatory measures and recommendations and has an in-built review and revision mechanism. The large number of ratifications of this Convention is persuasive evidence of the viability of the approach, although it may not be transferrable to other less international economic sectors.

[13] ILO (1996).

In adopting the Centenary Declaration on the Future of Work, the 2019 International Labour Conference requested the Governing Body "to consider, as soon as possible, proposals for including safe and healthy working conditions in the ILO's framework of fundamental principles and rights at work".[14] This does not necessarily call for amending the 1998 Declaration in some way.

One of the purposes of the 1998 Declaration was to achieve cohesion between the four categories of rights that it covers. With occupational safety and health, the next step might well be achieving more cohesion between existing standards and policy instruments. This could be done in several ways. A state of the art overview could lead into drafting a summary of principles which are common to existing instruments and can be linked to the ILO Constitution. The result could be either a Declaration or some other authoritative document, which could include a cross-reference to the 1998 Declaration. It would also be feasible to apply the "first-things-first" approach to determine action against the most dangerous but common hazards, rather in the way that the Social Floors Recommendation has done. The next recurrent discussion on occupational safety and health in the International Labour Conference would be a good place to propose decisions on future steps.

10 Where to Go Next with Standards?

The question has been often posed: to what extent has the International Labour Code already been completed? I would argue that the answer is, to some extent yes but there is always unfished business. In the last hundred years, we have covered virtually all of the basic elements of social justice as identified by the Constitution of the ILO. Yet we have to continue to adapt standards so that they maintain their relevance to structural, technological, economic and political changes in the world economy.

Work is a moving target, and the International Labour Code will never be complete in any case. Some of the early maritime labour standards covered occupations which no longer exist. Some of the early protective approaches to the work of women, such as prohibiting night work, have been replaced by demands for equality and safety. Furthermore, the necessary adaptation does not always need to be done—and in some cases cannot be done—by drafting new standards.

The potential of Recommendations is being harnessed. But this may not yet be sufficiently matched by the fact that Recommendations, as standards, are subject to overview by the standards supervisory mechanism. It would be entirely feasible to focus more on the information that can be obtained under Article 19 of the Constitution from not only Recommendations but also non-ratified Conventions.

[14] ILO, Resolution on the ILO Centenary Declaration for the Future of Work. International Labour Conference, 108th Session, Geneva, 21 June 2019.

We cannot run behind each change in labour conditions, trying to put up a new standard here or there. If we try this, by the time a Convention is adopted and effective, the issue may well have mutated into something else. What we need instead is a combination of standards and social dialogue, which is the singular contribution of the ILO over the last hundred years.

11 Standards in the Twenty-First Century

In the 1970s, the ILO adopted 23 Conventions. In the next decade, the number of Conventions was 16. In the 1990s, a total of 13 Conventions were adopted, and the number of stand-alone Recommendations increased. In the first decade of this millennium six Conventions were adopted. The second decade of the millennium has seen two Conventions, one Protocol and three stand-alone Recommendations. On the other hand, since 1998 the ILO has adopted three Declarations. These are not standards in the legal sense of the word, but one of their aims is to give instructions on how standards should be universally applied.

Thirty years ago, the combination of globalizing markets and the end of Cold War confrontation brought the issue of regulation and labour standards into new focus. Ever since this soul-searching started, standard-setting has been behaving differently.

In the first 20 years of this century, all the different instruments available to the ILO have been used. The latest Conventions are on such issues as domestic workers and violence at work. Recent stand-alone Recommendations deal with HIV/AIDS in the workplace, social protection floors, the informal economy and post-conflict transition to peace. The concept of Decent Work, launched by ILO Director-General Juan Somavia and pursued by his successor Guy Ryder has entered the body of standards. Through the Protocol to the 1930 Forced Labour Convention, the ILO covered the issue of human trafficking and also revised the Convention. In addition, in 2018 the Conference for the first time abrogated obsolete Conventions.

The work on international labour standards is not drying up. It is alive and well, and is adapting to the economic, social, political and technological changes of a globalized economy.

12 The State and the Social Partners

It is necessary to further reflect on the role of the state as well as the ILO's constituents, trade unions and employers. When in 2002 President Tarja Halonen came to Geneva to co-chair for the first time the ILO's World Commission on the Social Dimensions of Globalization, she defined the task in a simple and sensible way. The aim of the exercise should be to rehabilitate the social state. Since the technological changes of the 1980s and post-Cold War liberalization, with its shock therapies, the role of the state in guaranteeing basic welfare and services for its citizens has been under attack. Yet there are limits to how far the state can abandon or outsource its responsibilities. Crisis situations bring us rapidly to those limits.

All states of the European and Central Asian region have ratified the eight Conventions on Fundamental Principles and Rights at Work. This is a reaffirmation of the rule of law in their systems, which continue to aspire to the aims of a welfare state. Yet the economic, political and structural shocks of the last decade have had serious consequences. A feature of globalization is that prosperity and deprivation not only coexist but are increasing in all societies, whatever label we give to them.

One of the lessons of 20 years of technical cooperation on fundamental principles and rights is that their strength and sustainability depend on how they affect the individual and collective rights of workers and employers. For instance, freedom of association needs to be followed up by social dialogue and institution building. Eradicating discrimination calls for a competent labour inspectorate, gender equality and policies on migration and supporting different vulnerable groups. It also calls for a continuous effort to raise the social protection floors of societies. A case in point is the way in which health and safety measures have to rely on enabling workers to survey and intervene when conditions are inadequate and downright dangerous. This calls for competence-building for workers—and their right to consultation, negotiation and organization.

A significant proportion of labour and social issues are resolved through negotiations and social dialogue between the partners directly concerned. They make agreements which are legally binding on both parties. At times, in the discussion on what is binding and what is not, we seem to forget that voluntary bargaining produces legally binding outcomes.

International labour standards are negotiated, implemented and supervised through a process which is at times either bipartite or tripartite. With a combination of private and public actors and national and global pressures, participation by everyone is crucial. It is at workplaces where a universal principle becomes reality. Once we are clear about the principles, those directly concerned—employers and trade unions—are the ones who should find practical solutions to be applied. As before, it is in the self-interest of the state to support these processes with institutional and economic support.

Consequently, the worst thing that we can do is to saw off the branch of social dialogue. Our economic salvation and prosperity lies in the way in which rules—such as international labour standards—are implemented in practice. The state will continue to play a role in this, but we should increasingly enable the constituents of the ILO to determine how this is done. No central authority can have an overview and control of the endless amount of individual situations faced by employers, workers and local institutions. Here lies the real social responsibility of both management and labour.

13 Annex: A Timeline of the ILO and Globalization

13.1 The Founding of the ILO

The ILO was founded in 1919 in response to demands that clauses dealing with labour would be included in the Peace Treaty after the First World War. In this way the ILO was to provide the social dimension of the settlement after the Great War, which was supposed to end all wars.

The founding principles of the ILO were based on proposals made during and after the War by the trade unions of the Allied and Central Powers as well as neutral countries. They were particularly clearly expressed at conferences held in Leeds (1916) and Berne (1917 and 1919). Most of these goals were shared by Labour Parties and socially progressive intellectuals, academics and politicians of the time.

The Constitution of the ILO declared that universal peace was possible only through social justice. The basic aim of the ILO was to guarantee social justice through a minimum level of standards which would avoid competition between countries at the expense of labour conditions.

One of the founders of the ILO, the Belgian legal scholar Ernst Mahaim, explained the international dimension in the following way: "The concept of international legislation is from the outset opposed to that of absolutely unrestricted international competition.The idea is to allow *relative* freedom of competition, based on some degree of equality in costs of production; certain humanitarian requirements are to be taken out of the sphere of competition. This means that health, life and human dignity are regarded as benefits of supreme value. Humanitarian ideals are given precedence over considerations of economic profit."

Mahaim wrote these thoughts in the seminal history of the creation of the ILO, edited by James Shotwell in 1934. Shotwell—an influential negotiator on the American team in Paris in 1919—later recalled that the name of the "International Labour Organization" was something of a misnomer. What was created was an international economic organization to deal with labour problems.

The fact that different labour conditions affect trade had been discussed since the end of the slave trade and the beginning of industrialization. Labour issues were particularly urgent at the end of the First World War because of the Russian Revolution in 1917 and strikes by workers in many European countries. Tripartite cooperation thus became an acceptable alternative to conflict and revolution. This was supported by the non-revolutionary trade union movement, which was given a voice and a vote in decisions on laws and policies.

Throughout its history, the ILO has been confronted with the choice between revolt or reform. It has promoted the method of negotiations and incremental improvements as opposed to rejection and full-scale upheaval. Looking back today—with the experience of complex social, political and economic phenomena such as globalization—it has consistently searched to maximize the benefits of change while minimizing its negative consequences.

13.2 Albert Thomas 1920–1932

A priority of the French first Director of the ILO, Albert Thomas, was to establish the ILO as an actor in its own right in international economic policy making. He was only partly successful in this, due to reluctance on the part of governments and employers. However, he succeeded in getting the ILO to the table at important economic conferences in the 1920s, thus setting a pattern for ILO participation in world governance.

Thomas was more successful with promoting the rights of trade unions, which were often still viewed with suspicion, even hostility. Thomas supported integrating the unions in economic policy making, but he was criticized by employers, by the Soviet Union as well as by authoritarian and fascist political leaders.

The development of the new science of industrial relations further underlined the need to recognize and expand the role of trade unions. In his last report, in 1932, Albert Thomas explored the potential of both economic planning and industrial relations. However, it was difficult to defend the idea of planning because of the example of the Soviet Union, which remained a political threat and a challenge due to its stated support for revolutionary action by workers. Yet the ILO could show that, in times of crisis, the state had an important role in sustaining employment and production.

The United States stayed outside the ILO in 1919 although it had been instrumental in the peace negotiations. Yet some American businessmen were interested in engaging with it in studies on scientific management.

13.3 Depression and the New Deal 1932–1938

Unemployment was discussed regularly by the International Labour Conference and the ILO Governing Body. This focus soon widened from employment to the organization of production and the way in which economic policies were conducted.

With the Great Depression of the 1930s, the ILO's response was close to that of John Maynard Keynes. During the time of both Albert Thomas and his successor as Director, the British Harold Butler (1932–1938), the ILO supported going beyond unemployment insurance by public works programmes. These were a key element of Franklin D. Roosevelt's New Deal in the United States. They were also in line with the ILO's belief in an organized but democratic managed market economy, which helped convince the USA to join the ILO in 1934.

13.4 Interruption by War

The main contribution of the American Director of the ILO, John Winant (1938–1941) was to evacuate the ILO from Geneva to Montreal, Canada. The ILO faced an existential threat. Germany's ambitions included replacing the ILO by a fascist international labour organization.

The ILO was unable to achieve an in-depth conference discussion on tripartite cooperation before the Second World War interrupted its work. The experiences and lessons of war-time tripartite cooperation in Allied and neutral countries were examined at an extraordinary ILO Conference in 1941 in New York. Edward Phelan, the Irish Acting Director and later Director General (1941–1948) presented a report arguing why the ILO and tripartite cooperation needed to have a role for when the time came for reconstruction after the war.

The ILO's philosophy was in line with the democratic principles of the Allied countries. The Atlantic Charter of Roosevelt and Churchill, drafted in 1941, contained a reference to labour standards.

The 1944 International Labour Conference in Philadelphia made the ILO fully functional again. The Philadelphia Declaration strengthened the ILO's claim to be involved in all policy making. Tripartite cooperation was not limited to social questions; it extended to international economic policy as well as questions of war and peace. Eventually, the construction of European institutions involved consultative arrangements with employers and workers.

In this way the post-war role of the ILO was to provide the social dimension of reconstruction. In 1919–1939 tripartite cooperation had largely been a process at the international level, but now it became recognized as a national tool.

Despite the misgivings of the Soviet Union—due to the presence of free employers and independent trade unions—the ILO's status was confirmed as the first Specialized Agency of the United Nations family in 1946.

The notion of human rights was expressed after Philadelphia in the Universal Declaration of Human Rights which the United Nations adopted in 1948. The ILO adopted Conventions on freedom of association and the right to collective bargaining, forced labour and non-discrimination (including equal pay for work of equal value) in the 1940s and 1950s. If they had been adopted by the United Nations, employers and trade unions would not have had a role in drafting, promoting and supervising them.

13.5 The Golden Decades

The three decades following World War II are sometimes called "golden" or "glorious". This applied above all to Europe and the rest of the OECD area. The ILO was managed by the American David Morse (1948–1970), who had first-hand experience of German reconstruction. The global situation started to change rapidly due to the wave of decolonization, which transformed the composition of the ILO. The multilateral system of the United Nations differed radically from that of the League of Nations.

The Western market economy produced unprecedented growth, including in terms of incomes and social security for workers who increasingly formed the middle class of industrialized societies. While decolonization changed the global composition of states, it did not bring prosperity and security which would have been comparable to reconstruction in Europe and Japan. It created new needs and expectations for vast numbers of people, but it also provoked high levels of frustration.

The ILO participated from the beginning in the technical cooperation activities of the United Nations, which were aimed at helping the newly independent countries gain the necessary know-how to run their economies and societies. During the first two decades of its existence, the ILO had concentrated on international labour standards and knowledge and research. Now technical cooperation meant working physically on the ground, with governments, employers and trade unions in countries which had gained political independence but needed advice and help to manage their economy and society.

The human rights aspect of decolonisation was particularly marked in the case of *apartheid* in South Africa. African nations' opposition to *apartheid* almost blew up the 1963 International Labour Conference. It was the last vestige of colonial rule. In the 1920s and 1930s, Workers' Group members had pressured the ILO to take a stronger stand against forced labour in the colonies. The governments' general attitude had been to limit and regulate forced labour; the trade unions insisted successfully that the aim was to abolish it.

13.6 Rivalries Between Groups

Sovereignty was a significant concern for many of the newly independent countries. In many of them, the new leaders had participated in national liberation movements. They wanted assistance but not patronizing while the former imperial powers did not want to give up the benefits that years of dependence had generated. At the same time, the Cold War produced rivalries between the market economies and socialist systems.

The collective answer of the developing world was to aim at a New International Economic Order (NIEO). One of its cornerstones was sovereignty and strong government, which did not tolerate much internal opposition. Consequently, the NIEO was never accepted as such in the ILO where both employers and workers insisted on their autonomy and respect for international labour standards. In the ILO, the workers wanted to speak of a new international "economic and social order".

The workers generally agreed with the developing countries on economic policies, while on standards and rights they agreed with the industrialized democracies as well as with employers who opposed state intervention. Much of the support by employers for freedom of association in the ILO during the post-war reconstruction era was due to their insistence on free enterprise as opposed to communist state management.

13.7 Development or Rather Lack of It

In the newly independent countries, much of the body of international labour standards applied only for part of the economy. Independence alone and the growth of now indigenous activities did not produce jobs beyond a small circle. Industrialization thus increasingly proved not to be the solution. Neither the liberal market economy model nor the socialist development model could be successfully replicated in the developing world.

When the expected outcomes did not materialize, the ILO launched a World Employment Programme in the 1960s. This was a multidisciplinary approach to economic and social development problems, with an attempt at understanding the underlying factors of development.

At the same time, powerful new economic actors emerged on the world scene. The most significant were multinational enterprises, a factor with potential economic as well as political consequences. Some of them served the interests of their home countries, to the detriment of host governments. The most notable case was Chile, where a US multinational enterprise was involved in the coup d'état against president Salvador Allende in September 1973.

As a result, a new consensus emerged: there had to be both national and international guidance for the behaviour of multinational enterprises. The basic aim was to maximize the benefits of activities by international enterprises while minimizing their negative effects. This same principle has been later applied to technological change, structural adjustment—and to globalization.

Up to the end of the 1970s, the main hypothesis for future development was that of a mixed economy, with coexistence between private and public activities. In Sweden, plans were developed for wage earners' funds which would control much of the economy. The German practice of co-determination, *Mitbestimmung,* inspired different proposals for industrial democracy. This was not socialism; at most it was convergence.

The ILO, with capitalist, socialist and developing countries and different configurations of their workers and employers, tried to maintain a balance. The ideal outcome would have been convergence between the economic systems. But this did not happen. In fact, when capitalism and socialism "converged", this did not take place in the centre—where it might have been expected—but on the extremes of the market economy model.

13.8 Market Forces Reassert Themselves (1980–1989)

In the late 1970s the socially successful European economy started lagging behind. The same happened in Japan. A number of developing countries (such as Mexico) were confronted with debt crises. This led to an ideological conclusion: the industrialized countries and their economic models had allegedly developed rigidities because they had too much regulation for social and labour aims. It became fashionable again to speak of encouraging what John Maynard Keynes had critically called "the animal spirits" of the market.

This return to the markets was accompanied by significant technological change. This affected the way enterprises functioned. The model of management changed due to information and communication technology. Increased computerization enabled real time control of production in several locations in different countries. At the same time, traditional links were being cut between labour and management in the work collective.

Attempts to deal with what was labelled structural adjustment did not produce much tripartite consensus in the ILO. As Director-General (1974–1989), Francis Blanchard, from France, was successful with advancing technical cooperation with the developing world. He also brought China back into the sphere of ILO activities. However, he experienced more difficulties when the expectations and priorities of industrialized and developing countries differed increasingly from one another. At the same time, they were experiencing difficulties arising out of lack of employment and growth and persistent poverty.

The ILO was very much focused on the developing world while the basis of its activities in the industrialized countries weakened. The centralized state-led model of the communist countries was about to disappear. Since 1919 the ILO had played a significant role as an alternative to communism. Now, however, the threat of revolution seemed no longer to be there. Instead, consensus strengthened around a market economy model with more flexible social and labour rules.

In the industrialized countries, the post-World War II generation had come to believe that the ILO's basic task was to deal with the developing world. That was where employment growth and social stability were needed. However, the same problems that they tried to cope with now started to resurface at home.

The dynamics in the 1980s in Europe were dominated on the one side by Margaret Thatcher's United Kingdom, with a bitter miners' strike and lingering class conflict. At the same time, the internal market of the European Economic Community (later the EU) was built up by Commission President Jacques Delors through the introduction of social dialogue. Delors believed that a deepening internal market needed the support of the social partners, especially the trade unions. Margaret Thatcher was set on resurrecting a hard market economy despite trade union resistance. The beginnings of Brexit lie in these contradictory views about how to deal with labour and social questions.

Since the early days of the ILO, it had been accepted that social and employment concerns could legitimately slow down economic activity. In the 1980s, this belief was being revisited. The factors that affected it were the increasing role of private economic interests, especially MNEs, which were usually supported by the governments of their home countries. However, the MNEs grew more transnational and less dependent on national governments. The alternatives were limited, as neither the communist model nor centralized public management produced prosperity.

By the end of the Cold War, multinational enterprises had been recognized as a new and powerful international phenomenon. Attempts by the United Nations, the ILO and the OECD to regulate these multinational forces had shown the extent to which the rules of the game could not be enforced.

After three decades of economic, social and employment growth, the 1980s led to a rehabilitation of market forces and private entrepreneurship and a demand for more flexible social and labour standards. The process of setting up the ILO in 1919 had proved that international labour standards could be implemented only through national laws. There was no applicable jurisdiction over multinational entities. As the UN, the ILO and the OECD soon had to accept, the only way to get beyond non-binding recommendations was through follow-up mechanisms which provided for consultation and dialogue.

13.9 The Brave New Global Market Economy

The Berlin Wall started to crack at least a decade before it actually came down in November 1989. Parallel to the new technological and market-oriented policy in the West, the socialist countries had started realizing that their system no longer worked. In China, the reforms of the late 1970s led to inviting multinational enterprises to join partnerships between the market and social and political state control. The socialist countries of Europe, and Hungary in particular, sought a new balance by encouraging some market forces.

The systemic change led to both economic change and political democratization. However, the change went well beyond the dismantling of the European barriers between communism and the free market economies. Democratization took place almost everywhere. The *apartheid* system in South Africa was dismantled. Single-party systems in Francophone Africa came to an end, and former British colonies carried out multiparty elections. In Latin America there was a shift to the left, away from military rule.

On the economic side, the former socialist countries needed a radical new start. At the same time, the developing countries that entered the orbit of global trade wanted to gain maximum advantage in terms of what they had—one of them being abundant labour. The new global market economy came about through a rush to gain maximum advantage. One consequence of the changes was promotion of trade through the setting up of a new World Trade Organization in 1995. The expectations of the new participants in the global markets were vast. The general assumption was that there would be significant trade liberalization and no new trade restrictions.

Throughout the 1980s, the emphasis on the sovereignty of independent countries had run into conflict with ever clearer signs of interdependence. The phenomenon of multinational enterprises had increased awareness of the constraints created by private entities, which were increasingly outside state control. The liberalization of financial markets and capital movements increased this trend. The leading industrialized governments pursued pro-market policies which either by design or as a consequence diminished the state's role in the economy and narrowed the space for social and labour policies.

13.10 Search for Social Rules of Competition

In contrast to the endings of the world wars in 1919 or 1945, there was no peace treaty when the Cold War evaporated, no settlement, and no social dimension. This was not on the agenda of the United Nations or other international bodies dealing with transition from state controlled to market economies and the opening of markets. The closest the world community came to that were the negotiations for creating a real World Trade Organization. There was only limited scope for social concerns in the process that led to the WTO in 1995.

In the industrialized countries, employment and prosperity of workers were being threatened by the new and unregulated operation of the global production system. When walls came down, what appeared on the other side was that the problems that the ILO had wrestled with throughout its lifetime were still there: child labour, forced labour, discrimination and limitations on freedom of association. Not only were they there: the trade of several countries was boosted by unacceptable labour standards.

The result was a discussion on a possible social clause in trade agreements so that trade liberalization would be conditioned by respect for certain fundamental labour standards. There were different views on whether this should be managed by the WTO or the ILO, or both, and how.

Michel Hansenne, from Belgium, who was Director-General of the ILO 1989–1999, presented to the 1974 International Labour Conference a report which recognized the new context and explored ways to deal with it. He disagreed with the idea of a social clause in the WTO but maintained that the social dimension of trade liberalization could be encouraged. The immediate focus was on trade, but the agenda was soon redirected into a more general discussion on globalization. It was at this stage that the concept of globalization entered the multilateral vocabulary.

The ILO has always striven to find a negotiated, consensus-based solution to situations which are inherently conflictual. Since the early 1990s the ILO had increasingly tried to help put an end to child labour, which had become an acute issue due to the opening of world markets. There were popular calls for banning the imports of all goods produced by children or boycotts of imports from countries which did nothing against child labour.

In stressing technical cooperation to eliminate child labour, to monitor production and education and training as an alternative for children who had not yet finished their basic schooling, the ILO acted in exactly the way in which labour standards and tripartite cooperation were used as an alternative to revolutions and disruption. In 1919 there had been attempts to export (and import) revolutions. This time the question was of trade, which was seen to undermine incomes and minimum safety for workers.

The WTO stated categorically that labour standards were a matter for the ILO and called on all Member States to assist the ILO in setting and supervising them. This led to a Declaration on Fundamental Principles and Rights at Work, adopted by the International Labour Conference in June 1998. The Declaration determined that every member of the ILO had to respect the principles of freedom of association and the right to collective bargaining, abolition of forced labour, elimination of child labour and non-discrimination in employment and occupation (including equal remuneration).

The novelty of the Declaration was that it concerned not only those countries that had ratified the Conventions of these four human rights categories. The obligations extended to all. Those who had no legal obligations through ratifications had the obligation, arising out of the ILO Constitution, to strive to realize the principles. Reports were requested and examined from all countries. This led to debate, especially on China, the Gulf States and the United States. In addition, the Declaration recommended technical cooperation as the way to resolve shortcomings in the application of fundamental standards. This opened the road to using technical cooperation on a large scale for human rights problems in the labour field. In general, the countries concerned recognized that technical cooperation could be a real alternative to trade or other boycotts.

13.11 Decent Work

The notion of Decent Work was developed by the Chilean Director-General of the ILO, Juan Somavia, in his first report upon taking office in 1999. The aim was not to change the aims of the ILO but to repackage them. The ILO budget had expanded to 39 major programmes, and Somavia concluded that an organization with so many priorities had no priorities at all. He cut the number to four: employment, social protection, standards, and social dialogue. "Decent Work" was a convenient way to express these aims—but especially after Amartya Sen's recognition of it as a development paradigm at the 1999 International Labour Conference, it became the framework for managing and carrying out ILO activities.

Decent Work remains a shorthand way of expressing the ILO's purpose. It also underlines the interdependence between actions in these fields. To succeed in the sustainable promotion of Decent Work, it was necessary to engage all four areas of action. Gradually the notion of Decent Work became accepted by the multilateral system, including the United Nations.

13.12 The Globalization Commission 2002–2004

The international dimension of Decent Work—or in other words, the link between decent work and globalization—was examined in depth by a tripartite World Commission on the Social Dimension of Globalization, co-chaired by Presidents Tarja Halonen of Finland and Benjamin Mkapa of Tanzania. The Commission surveyed the full range of social and labour issues. It built on the traditional aim of maximizing benefits and minimizing negative effects. One of its messages was that, to be acceptable, globalization must be fair—and it must be seen to be fair.

The World Commission also commented on the fundamental principles and rights at work of the 1998 Declaration, pushing them one step further. While the Declaration had noted that these rights should not be used for protectionist purposes, the Commission added that nor should denial of these rights be used to gain competitive advantage.

In 2008, this principle was included in the ILO Declaration on Social Justice for a Fair Globalization. This Declaration was designed to be the compass for promotion of fair globalization based on Decent Work.

13.13 The Financial Crisis and the Global Jobs Pact

The 2008 Declaration underlines that the four objectives of the ILO—the objectives of Decent Work—are inseparable, interrelated and mutually supportive. This probably was the strongest recognition of interdependence up to that date in the official positions of the ILO. Furthermore, it created a follow-up in the International Labour Conference. Henceforth each strategic objective would be regularly and in turn discussed by the Conference. The aim was to determine how the issues have developed, how ILO programmes were working, and what improvements—including new or revised international labour standards—would be needed.

So far this system of recurrent items has led to adoption of a Recommendation on Social Protection Floors; a protocol against Trafficking of people for the Forced Labour Convention 1930 (No. 29); and an agreement to work further on labour conditions in global supply chains. In other words, the different negative aspects of globalization are being tackled by the ILO with concrete normative action and technical cooperation.

The era of globalization provoked tripartite discussions which, in turn, led to instruments and action on which there was broad consensus. A consensus was reached on the Global Jobs Pact, adopted at the International Labour Conference in 2009, which included a Jobs Summit of several Presidents. However, it did not lead to extensive follow-up measures. This is all the more regrettable, as the initiative came from employers—especially from national employers who had started feeling the pressures of the financial crisis. Yet one consequence has been that, since 2009, the ILO has regularly been invited to participate in the G20 Leaders' Summit meetings. The Labour and Social Affairs Ministers of the G20 group also meet, and they consult with international employers' organizations and trade unions.

There is a difference in the approach of the Employers' and Workers' Groups. For the workers, the natural model of a follow-up has been the international labour standards system, which can reach out to legal or at least semi-legal conclusions concerning violations of rights. The employers' vision generally is more of systems of information and consultation, without sanctions or legal obligations. It is not surprising that, for a hundred years, the workers have been advocating adoption of Conventions whereas, for the employers, the preferred form of instrument has been a Recommendation.

13.14 The Future of Work and the Centenary Declaration

Juan Somavia's successor, Guy Ryder from Great Britain, was elected Director-General of the ILO in 2012. He has directed much attention to the future of work. A new tripartite Global Commission—set up to study the topic—made its recommendations in January 2019. They were the basis for the Centenary Declaration, adopted by the International Labour Conference in June 2019.

In that Declaration, the word "globalization" is mentioned only twice. Does this mean that priorities have shifted? The context is more important than the frequency of mention. The Declaration is quite honest in asserting the basis of the world economy as it has developed over the last three decades. It supports the private sector as "a principal source of economic growth and job creation" while the public sector is "a significant employer and provider of quality public services".

This could be seen as the definite end to a period of competition between private and public development models. In this context, Decent Work appears as the key to sustainable development, conflict resolution and prevention, and cohesive nation building. In the context of globalization, the Centenary Declaration reaches out to one of the main Constitutional assertions, namely that the failure of any country to treat its workers humanely is an obstacle to all other countries which desire to do so. Fittingly, the Declaration weaves together the threads from over one hundred years to produce a narrative which, while not new, is the result of continuous review and updating.

In this light, it is logical that after the years of adjusting the principles of social justice to the challenges of a globalized world, it is important to determine what kind of concrete action needs to be taken. The Conference of 2019 adopted a new Convention on Violence and Harassment at Work. This Convention (No. 190) reminds us that freedom from violence and harassment at work is a human right, and in working life the rules have to cover everyone, irrespective of the contractual form of their employment. In addition, the Conference asked for further strengthening of the right to workplaces with guaranteed proper conditions of occupational safety and health.

This can be seen as a logical trajectory for the ILO. A hundred years ago the ILO was first preoccupied by such questions as hours of work, minimum age for employment, and protection against unemployment as well as conditions before and after active years of work. The brutality of World War II highlighted the role of international labour standards for democracy, thus promoting recognition of universal human rights. This was followed by decolonization and technical assistance and, later on, the search for social principles of globalization.

The principles have been clarified but have not changed. Their application must be adapted to economic and social realities—both national and international. The ILO would be well advised to move ahead with as concrete application as possible of the principles which were for the first time adopted in its Constitution in 1919 and recognized as guidelines for social justice ever since. The rule of law must be maintained as the basic framework. Within it, any consensus at the parliamentary and macro-economic levels needs to be translated into specific agreements and real action at the national, sectoral and local level. Tripartite cooperation and collective bargaining play a crucial role here. This is the way to promote universal principles at the level of workplaces and enterprises—and society in general.

References

ILO (1996) Report VI (1) Child labour – targeting the intolerable, Sixth item on the agenda. International Labour Conference, 86th Session, Geneva, 1998

Morse DA (1969) The origin and evolution of the I.L.O. and its role in the world community. Cornell University – New York State School of Industrial and Labor Relations, Ithaca

OECD (1996) Trade and labour standards, COM/DEELSA/TD/ 96(8). Directorate for Education, Employment, Labour and Social Affairs and the Trade Directorate, Paris

Office of the United States Trade Representative (2019) Ongoing country reviews: Georgia, petitioner: AFL–CIO, basis for petition: workers rights (USTR 2013-0009). Available at: www.ustr.gov/issue-areas/preference-programs/generalized-system-preferences-gsp/current-reviews/ongoing-country. Accessed 4 May 2020

Smith A (2012) Wealth of nations. Wordsworth Editions Ltd, Ware

Tapiola K (2018) The teeth of the ILO: the impact of the declaration on fundamental principles and rights at work. International Labour Office, Geneva

UN (1995) Report of the World Summit for Social Development (Copenhagen, 1995)

Kari Tapiola has worked as a journalist, a national and international trade union official, and an international civil servant. In 1996–2010 he was Deputy Director-General of the International Labour Office in Geneva. Since retiring he has continued advising the ILO and participating in technical cooperation activities on fundamental principles and rights at work.

How to Improve Monitoring and Enforcement of International Labour Standards?

Bernd Waas

Contents

1 Introduction

International labour standards are important and deserve every effort to ensure monitoring and enforcement. The fundamental objective of the ILO, which owes its existence to the Treaty of Versailles and is therefore directly linked to the tragedy of World War I, is set out in the preamble to the Constitution. Its first sentence reads: "In the long run, world peace can only be built on social justice". Who would deny that today? A certain reorientation of the goals of the ILO then took place, under the impression of the Second World War, with the Philadelphia Declaration of 1944. Its much quoted first principle is: "Work is not a commodity". This statement seems more relevant today than ever. Global value chains, the increasing importance of artificial intelligence and the expanding platform economy clearly open up opportunities, but at the same time they are accompanied by considerable risks for working people. These risks should remind us of our task to ensure that work does not become a commodity in the future.

B. Waas (✉)
Goethe University, Frankfurt am Main, Germany
e-mail: waas@jur.uni-frankfurt.de

T. Halonen, U. Liukkunen (eds.), *International Labour Organization and Global Social Governance*, https://doi.org/10.1007/978-3-030-55400-2_4

To achieve this, two things are needed: first, the existence of international standards that take into account the realities of current labour markets, and second, adequate monitoring and effective enforcement of those standards. This chapter is devoted to the issue of monitoring and enforcement. It starts by outlining the existing system (Sect. 2) and then looks at how better monitoring and enforcement could be ensured in the future (Sect. 3). Three issues will be addressed in this regard: improved cooperation between international organisations and, in particular, enhanced dialogue between courts and other supervisory bodies; the EU's contribution to the enforcement of international labour standards; and the role of the private sector in the monitoring and enforcement of these standards. Let us start with a stocktaking exercise.

2 State of Play

2.1 The Current System

Within the ILO, monitoring and enforcement of international labour standards have changed over time. The system in place today works well on balance. However, the system is quite complex, at least at first sight: different bodies are responsible for monitoring standards and there are specific as well as general monitoring mechanisms. This cannot be set out here in detail. Instead, I will limit myself to a brief sketch.

If there is a possible violation of freedom of association, the Committee on Freedom of Association (CFA) will be responsible. So far, the Committee has commented on about 3200 cases.[1] The Committee was established in 1951 by the Governing Body of the ILO. This decision was based on an agreement between the ILO and the UN that a specific procedure should be established to ensure effective monitoring of Member States' obligations to ensure freedom of association.[2] The Committee's task is to determine "whether any given legislation or practice complies with the principles of freedom of association and collective bargaining laid down in the relevant Conventions".[3] The establishment of the CFA reflects the fundamental importance that the ILO attaches to these guarantees. The Committee on Freedom of Association has a tripartite structure and its members are representatives of the governments of the ILO member states as well as representatives of workers and employers. The Chairman of the Committee is independent.

In addition to the Committee on Freedom of Association, there are two other main players. As part of the general monitoring process, these actors have shared

[1] Cf. ILO (2018).

[2] Cf. Beaudonnet (2010), p. 73.

[3] ILO, Special procedures for the examination in the International Labour Organization of complaints alleging violations of freedom of association – Annex 1 (no. 14).

responsibilities: The Committee of Experts on the Application of Convention and Recommendations (CEACR or Committee of Experts) and the Conference Committee on the Application of Standards (CAS). General monitoring is based on reports which, under the Constitution of the ILO, the members have to submit at regular intervals.[4] The report must contain the following information: an indication of the relevant laws, regulations and other legal sources (including copies); exceptions and the like, where permitted by the relevant Convention; information on the implementation of each individual provision of a Convention in national law; details of the legal effects of ratification of the Convention under national law; responses to possible opinions of the Committee of Experts; information on the bodies responsible for enforcement of a Convention; relevant decisions by courts and administrative authorities; details of any results of assistance or advice given in the context of ILO technical cooperation projects; a general assessment of the application of the Convention (including extracts from official reports, statistics, details of violations, prosecutions, and the like).[5] In addition, the reports must be accompanied by copies of observations made by employers' and workers' organisations.[6]

As already mentioned, the task of monitoring standards is carried out on the one hand by the Committee of Experts and on the other hand by the Conference Committee on the Application of Standards. Both committees are strictly separated, but work together. There is, however, a clear division of roles. This is explained by the different structures and tasks of the two bodies: the conference committee has a tripartite structure and bases its decisions partly on aspects of opportunity. The Committee of experts consists of independent experts. It carries out its assessment exclusively from a legal point of view. This background is necessary in order to understand that the Committee of Experts has repeatedly invoked in its reports a "spirit of mutual respect, cooperation and responsibility"[7]: the wording takes account of the joint responsibility of the two institutions for monitoring international standards, but at the same time makes it clear that the Committee attaches importance to its independence.

Anyone who deals with future issues should also consider the past. This also applies to the question of future monitoring and enforcement of international standards: In the early days of the ILO, there was no system for monitoring standards. It was not until 1926 that, against the background of an increasing number of

[4] See Art. 22 of the Constitution of the ILO: "Each of the Members agrees to make an annual report to the International Labour Office on the measures which it has taken to give effect to the provisions of Conventions to which it is a party. These reports shall be made in such form and shall contain such particulars as the Governing Body may request."

[5] Cf. ILO (2019a), p. 25 et seq.

[6] Cf. Art. 23(2) of the Constitution of the ILO: "Each Member shall communicate to the representative organizations recognized for the purpose of article 3 copies of the information and reports communicated to the Director-General in pursuance of articles 19 and 22."

[7] See, e.g., Committee of Experts on the Application of Conventions and Recommendations (2018), para 13.

ratifications, the ILO was to establish such a system.[8] Two institutions were formed at that time: The Conference Committee and—initially only on a temporary basis—the Committee of Experts, which met for the first time in 1927 (with eight members). As already indicated above, the (tripartite) Conference Committee was always understood to be a political body. On the other hand, the Committee of Experts should ensure an independent legal analysis[9] and, in particular, uncover different interpretations of the provisions of the Convention in the Member States.[10] The Committee should include its observations in a "technical report" to be submitted to the Director. Great care was taken to set narrow limits for the Committee: Under no circumstances should the Committee be allowed to subpoena government representatives. It should also limit its work entirely to the information provided by governments.[11] From the outset, there were concerns that the new committee could undermine members' sovereign rights and interfere in other ILO bodies' reserved areas. These concerns were allayed, in particular, by emphasising that the committee should in no way be a court-like body.[12] A fundamental reform then took place as a result of far-reaching changes to the ILO Constitution in 1946, which greatly expanded the reporting obligations of its members. As a result, the mandates both of the Conference Committee and of the Committee of Experts were extended. The task of the Committee of Experts is to indicate to what extent the legislation and practice of each member is in conformity with the ratified conventions and to what extent the members have fulfilled their norm-related obligations under the ILO Constitution. The Committee of Experts should serve as an "intermediate stage in

[8] Cf. Resolution concerning the methods by which the Conference can make use of the reports submitted under Article 408 of the Treaty of Versailles, submitted by the Committee on Article 408. In: ILO (1926) International Labour Conference, Record of Proceedings, 8th Session, Geneva, 26 May–5 June 1926, p. 429.

[9] Cf. ILO (1926) International Labour Conference, Record of Proceedings, 8th Session, Geneva, 26 May–5 June 1926, p. 396: "Further, it may be observed that the Conference and its Committees are essentially deliberative and political bodies, composed of the representatives of various interests, national or occupational, and that in general such bodies are not the best suited for the technical work now under consideration." Cf. also, p. 398: "The Committee of Experts might therefore be, not a committee set up directly by the Conference, but a committee created by the Director, on the instructions of the Conference and with the approval of the Governing Body, to carry out a particular task in view of the technical preparation of one part of the work of the Conference. The Conference itself would conserve its proper political functions, but it would be advised as to the facts by this technical expert Committee, and it would, either directly, or through one of its own Committees, decide upon its attitude and upon what appropriate action it might take or indicate."

[10] Ibid., p. 401: "Its examination will certainly reveal cases in which different interpretations of the provisions of Conventions appear to be adopted in different countries. The Committee should call attention to such cases."

[11] Ibid., p. 401: "[…] there is and can be no question of convoking Governments or their representatives before the proposed Committee, which would base its reports entirely upon the information which the States have undertaken in ratifying the Convention, to supply."

[12] Ibid., p. 405: "It was agreed […] that the Committee of experts would have no judicial capacity nor would it be competent to give interpretations of the Conventions not to decide in favour of one interpretation rather than of another."

the monitoring process" and prepare the review of the application of the Conventions by the Conference Committee.[13]

The Committee of Experts, currently composed of 20 independent members, meets once a year for some 3 weeks to review the reports submitted by members. The meetings of the Committee are not open to the public. Committee deliberations and documents are confidential.[14] The Office provides the Committee members with considerable support in fulfilling their tasks. In fact, one simply cannot praise the office and its staff enough for its input. The work of the Committee of Experts results in opinions, for which a distinction is made between observations and direct requests. Observations are usually used in serious or long-standing cases of non-compliance. They are included in the report of the Committee, which is submitted to the Conference Committee each year in June of the following year and is also published as part of the Annual Report. Direct requests, on the other hand, are sent directly to the government concerned. They are not included in the annual report.[15] Unlike direct requests, observations are normally used in serious or protracted cases of non-compliance. In this regard, so-called "special notes", which are traditionally referred to as footnotes, are of particular importance. In the case of a so-called single footnote, the Committee requests an earlier report from the government. A double footnote even asks a government to provide comprehensive and detailed information at the next International Labour Conference. In answering the question whether one or the other type of footnote should be considered, the Committee takes into account, among other things, the seriousness of the problem (in particular with regard to the interests involved); the persistence of the problem; the duration and urgency of the situation; and the type of reaction by a Member State.[16]

The comments of the Committee of Experts form the basis for the work of the Conference Committee. The Conference Committee discusses problems arising in the implementation of agreements and recommendations on the basis of the report submitted by the Committee of Experts. Most importantly, the comments of the Committee of Experts form the basis for selection of cases to be further discussed at the International Labour Conference, which takes place every year. In practice, the Conference Committee selects approximately 20 cases each year for closer inspection. Since 2012, discussion of these cases by the International Labour Conference Committee has started with cases which have been given a double footnote by the Committee of Experts.[17]

It should not be concealed that the mandate of the Expert Committee is not uncontroversial within the ILO. Dispute was sparked by the fact that the Committee derives a right to strike from Convention No 87, although that right is not explicitly

[13] International Labour Office (1947) Minutes of the 103rd Session of the Governing Body, Geneva, December 1947, p. 169 et seq.

[14] Cf. ILO (2019a), p. 35 et seq.

[15] Cf. Ibid., p. 36.

[16] Committee of Experts on the Application of Conventions and Recommendations (2018), para 45 et seq.

[17] Cf. ILO (2019a), p. 38 et seq.

mentioned in the Convention. It has to be said, without any accusation of guilt, that the dispute is highly regrettable because it creates the danger that the credibility and authority of the supervisory bodies could be damaged. The Committee of Experts itself takes the following view with regard to its mandate:

> The Committee of Experts on the Application of Conventions and Recommendations is an independent body established by the International Labour Conference and its members are appointed by the ILO Governing Body. It is composed of legal experts charged with examining the application of ILO Conventions and Recommendations by ILO member States. The Committee of Experts undertakes an impartial and technical analysis of how the Conventions are applied in law and practice by member States, while cognizant of different national realities and legal systems. In doing so, it must determine the legal scope, content and meaning of the provisions of the Conventions. Its opinions and recommendations are non-binding, being intended to guide the actions of national authorities. They derive their persuasive value from the legitimacy and rationality of the Committee's work based on its impartiality, experience and expertise. The Committee's technical role and moral authority is well recognized, particularly as it has been engaged in its supervisory task for more than 90 years, by virtue of its composition, independence and its working methods built on continuing dialogue with governments taking into account information provided by employers' and workers' organizations. This has been reflected in the incorporation of the Committee's opinions and recommendations in national legislation, international instruments and court decisions.[18]

2.2 *Deficiencies*

It was stated above that the standards monitoring system works. This does not mean, however, that there is no room for improvement. For example, it is clear that many Member States are not meeting their reporting obligations, are not meeting them on time, or are not meeting them to the required extent. The report of the Committee of Experts for the year 2018 reports with concern the high number of reports that were not received on time so that cases had to be deferred.[19] At the same time, the workload of the Committee of Experts and the Office is enormous. As a result, a considerable number of reports cannot be dealt with promptly by the Committee. Instead, their examination is postponed to the following year. To remedy this or at least mitigate the adverse consequences is an ongoing task that has led to a number of changes, particularly in recent times. For instance, the decision was taken a while ago to extend the so-called "reporting cycles".[20] There have also been some reforms

---

[18] Cf., e.g., Committee of Experts on the Application of Conventions and Recommendations (2018), para 19.

[19] Ibid., para 25 et seq.

[20] The Governing Body of the ILO decided some time ago to extend the reporting cycle to 6 years. See International Labour Office (2018) Fifth Item on the Agenda – The Standards Initiative: Implementing the workplan for strengthening the supervisory system Progress report. In: Decisions adopted by the Governing Body at its 334th Session and outcomes of the discussions, Geneva, 25 October–8 November 2018.

of a more technical nature, such as increased use of electronic tools or the creation of teams of members of the Committee of Experts or the grouping of Conventions for the purpose of examination by the Committee members.

In all this, it should also be borne in mind that the Committee of Experts does have considerable room for manoeuvre in its work as the committee has no rules of procedure. Rather, the committee itself decides on its own "working methods". To this end, a subcommittee was set up in 2001 to deal in detail with issues relating to the organisation of the work of the Committee. In practice, all members of the Committee of Experts attend meetings of the Subcommittee, which may serve as an indication that working methods are understood to be of utmost importance.

3 Questions for the Future

The problem of monitoring and enforcing international standards is (almost) as old as the standards themselves. However, this task will not be easier to accomplish. With the rapid advance of digitisation, work is becoming a shy deer, making it increasingly difficult not only to regulate, but also to monitor and enforce the relevant standards. The fact that technological advances also offer some opportunities in this respect—the Global Commission in its report refers, among other things, to the virtues of blockchain technology[21]—is a rather weak consolation. What is certain is that international standards will increasingly aim to regulate transnational issues and that, accordingly, cooperation between the ILO member states across borders will be necessary in the enforcement of these standards, as is already the case today, for example, within the framework of the Maritime Labour Convention of 2006, where the enforcement regime is based on shared enforcement of maritime labour conditions by flag and port States.[22]

3.1 Cooperation Between All International Organisations

Bur monitoring of standards requires more, namely ever-intensive cooperation between all international organisations. The first step should be to develop an approach that goes beyond individual policy areas to ensure that efforts in one area are not thwarted by efforts in another. Rather than that, synergies should be sought.

---

[21] ILO (2019b), p. 44.

[22] See Title 5 of the Maritime Labour Convention, 2006.

3.1.1 A Comprehensive Policy Approach

Such fruitful cooperation already exists on many levels. The OECD deserves a positive mention in this respect.[23] Here there are examples not only of the fact that core labour standards have been given additional legitimacy, but also of the fact that independent pressure has been exerted to urge states to comply with labour standards. In one case, for example, membership of the organisation was made conditional on the particular state showing greater respect for freedom of association. The OECD Guidelines for Multinational Enterprises in its Commentary section explicitly acknowledge the work of the ILO by expressly stating that it is the ILO which is "the competent body to set and deal with international labour standards, and to promote fundamental rights at work". The Guidelines, the text goes on to say, "have a role to play in promoting observance of these standards and principles among multinational enterprises".[24]

While in the relationship between the ILO and the OECD the idea of cooperation is predominant, the picture is less positive when it comes to other international organisations which are also becoming increasingly involved in the social arena.[25] The relationship between the IMF and the World Bank and the latter's position with regard to international labour standards has been relatively well researched in the literature. There, it has repeatedly been pointed out that compliance with international labour standards is in a certain tension with the deregulation of labour markets, which is predominantly favoured by both the World Bank and the IMF. In addition, a number of studies suggest that structural adjustment programmes fostered by the two institutions have come with a decline of labour rights protection in the countries concerned.[26]

The relationship between the ILO and WTO and the importance of international standards in the area of free trade agreements is a chapter in itself. It is well known that attempts to integrate "social clauses" into such agreements within the framework of the WTO have so far been unsuccessful.[27] This is mainly due to the fact that the member states assess such clauses very differently. Developed countries are usually in favour. Developing countries, however, argue that the attempt to bring labour issues into the WTO is actually a bid by industrial nations to undermine the comparative advantage associated with lower social standards and that efforts to bring labour standards into the arena of multilateral trade negotiations are little more than a smokescreen for protectionism. At the same time, there is a fear among them that the proposed standards may be too ambitious. That a consensus could emerge in the near future seems unlikely. But perhaps we can still allow ourselves a

[23] Cf. in this regard Thouvenin (2015), p. 385.

[24] OECD (2011), p. 37. On the other hand, the revised Tripartite Declaration of Principles concerning Multinational Enterprises and Social Policy includes a reference to the OECD Guidelines.

[25] Cf. Chen (2018), p. 184.

[26] Cf. Ebert (2018), pp. 273–274 with further references (footnote 3); see also Ebert (2015), p. 124.

[27] Cf. Stoll (2018), pp. 11–27.

brief dream and imagine for a moment that progress could indeed be made within the framework of the WTO on international standards whose justification as such must be completely undisputed. Think, for example, of proposals from legal circles aiming at establishing a joint ILO-WTO implementation mechanism to combat child labour. It has been suggested in the literature that such a mechanism in certain cases such as export-related child labour could be subject to dispute settlement resulting in trade measures as measures of last resort. In addition to the intergovernmental dispute settlement system, there would also be a private complaints mechanism where non-governmental organisations on behalf of children could bring certain complaints against companies and governments. Panels would include ILO experts and decisions would be based on UN and ILO jurisprudence. Complaints against governments could result in dispute resolution ending with trade measures.[28] If only such a scenario could come true!

In any case, any attempt to bring about more intensive cooperation is worthwhile. In view of this, one can only endorse the Global Commission on the Future of Work. It writes in its report:

> We recommend in particular the establishment of more systemic and substantive working relations between the World Trade Organization (WTO), the Bretton Woods institutions and the ILO. There are strong, complex and crucial links between trade, financial, economic and social policies. The success of the human- centred growth and development agenda we propose depends heavily on coherence across these policy areas.[29]

There is nothing to add to that.

3.1.2 Enhanced Dialogue Between Supervisory Bodies

However, it is not only international organisations as such that are called upon to intensify cooperation, but also the courts and other international supervisory bodies set up to monitor international standards should enter into intensified dialogue with each other. In particular, these bodies would be well advised not to lead a life of their own, but also to orient themselves to findings by others in the performance of their supervisory tasks. In this regard, one could take a leaf out of the book of the practice of the European Court of Human Rights (ECtHR).[30] In 2008, for example, the Court, in its decision in *Demir and Baykara* (on the establishment of a trade union by employees of a municipality), expressly stated that in interpreting the provisions of the ECHR, the Court "can and must take into account elements of international law other than the Convention, the interpretation of such elements by competent organs, and the practice of European States reflecting their common values". The Court went on to say: "The consensus emerging from specialised international instruments and from the practice of Contracting States may constitute a

28 See Humbert (2018), pp. 93–109.

29 ILO (2019b), p. 14.

30 For more details, see Teklè (2018), p. 236; Waas (2019), pp. 123–147.

relevant consideration for the Court when it interprets the provisions of the Convention in specific cases."[31] In doing so, the ECtHR orientates itself not least on the rulings of the CFA and CEACR. All this does not mean that differences between the different panels should not be taken into account. The ECtHR itself at times has emphasised differences between the Court of Justice on the one hand and ILO supervisory bodies on the other. According to the ECtHR, ILO supervisory bodies have "to review the relevant domestic law in the abstract", whereas the court has to decide on a concrete legal dispute.[32] In spite of these differences, the Court takes the rulings of ILO supervisory bodies into consideration. In the *Enerji Yapi-Yol Sen* case, for example, in 2009 the Court recognised the right to strike for civil servants by, among other things, referring to the ILO supervisory bodies.[33] The most recent example of a reference by the ECtHR to the findings of the Committee of Experts is the decision of the Court of Justice in the *Ognovenko* case concerning the legality of strikes in Russian rail transport. In this respect, the Court recalls that the Committee does not regard the railway sector as an "essential service" in which strikes could be banned and that the Committee has for some time been calling on Russia to ensure that railway workers could exercise their right to strike.[34]

Basically, the same applies to the European Committee of Social Rights. This will not be substantiated in detail here. Instead, I would like to take the liberty of quoting Monika Schlachter, a former long-standing member of the ECSR. In a recent article, she came to the following conclusion:

> The ILO Committees [...], the ECHR and the ECSR are increasingly orienting themselves towards the goal of greater convergence in the concretisation and development of social rights by using the historically close link between social protection rights for their interpretation. This applies in particular to the interpretation results developed by the ILO monitoring bodies, which are used at both international and national level to concretise social rights.[35]

The CJEU stands in striking contrast to this. For instance, in the "famous" *Laval* and *Viking* rulings, the CJEU derived a right to strike from, among others, ILO Convention No. 87, although that right is not expressly mentioned in the Convention.[36] In this respect, it would have been self-evident to refer to the stance

---

[31] European Court of Human Rights (Grand Chamber), *Demir and Baykara v. Turkey* (App. No. 34503/97), Judgment, 12 November 2008, para 85.

[32] European Court of Human Rights (Fourth Section), *National Union of Rail, Maritime and Transport Workers v. The United Kingdom* (App. No. 31045/10), Judgment, 8 April 2014, para 95.

[33] European Court of Human Rights (Third Section), *Enerji Yapi-Yol Sen v. Turkey* (App. No. 68959/01) (*Enerji Yapi-Yol Sen/Türkei*), Judgment, 21 April 2009, para 24.

[34] European Court of Human Rights (Third Section *Ognovenko v. Russia* (App. No. 44873/09), Judgment, 20 November 2018, para 22 et seq.

[35] Schlachter (2019), pp. 491–494.

[36] CJEU (Grand Chamber), *Laval un Partneri Ltd v Svenska Byggnadsarbetareförbundet, Svenska Byggnadsarbetareförbundets avdelning 1, Byggettan and Svenska Elektrikerförbundet* (Case C-341/05), Judgment, 18 December 2007, para 90; CJEU (Grand Chamber), *International Transport Workers' Federation and Finnish Seamen's Union v Viking Line ABP and OÜ Viking Line Eesti* (Case C-438/05), Judgement, 11 December 2007, para 43.

of the Committee of Experts, which in fact affirms that very right. However, this is precisely what the CJEU did not do.

3.2 *The Role of the EU*

A look at the limited reception of international labour law directs attention to the European Union as such. What could the EU do to help enforce international standards? Let us dream for a moment and ask: Would anything perhaps be gained if the EU as such were to join the ILO and then ratify all the ILO conventions? The question seems bold, almost absurd. But to raise such questions is the privilege of the academic. Nevertheless, the idea should not be pursued here. Apart from the question whether accession really would have predominantly positive effects on the enforcement of standards, there would be so many legal and political obstacles to accession that one can immediately say goodbye to that idea. By contrast, it would seem somewhat more realistic to open ILO conventions to future accession by regional organisations such as the EU. There would even be a role model for that. For the first time in a human rights convention with worldwide validity, the Convention on the Rights of Persons with Disabilities of 2006 allows "regional integration organizations"[37] to also accede to the convention.[38] And indeed, the EU is the first international organisation that made use of the possibility of accession and ratified it, in 2011.[39] Ever since, the CJEU has repeatedly used the Convention to interpret Union law.[40]

Instead of binding itself externally, however, the EU could also enter into a kind of "self-commitment". There would also be role models for this. In fact, there are already two directives which, by taking over a large part of the content of a convention, produce an almost identical result to ratification by the EU. Both directives concern issues of maritime labour law. To begin with, Directive 2009/13/EC was adopted to implement an agreement between the relevant social partners in the industry, which for its part largely adopts the 2006 ILO Maritime Labour Convention.[41] As a result, the Directive incorporates large parts of the Maritime

---

[37] See Art. 44(1) of the Convention on the Rights of Persons with Disabilities: "'Regional integration organization' shall mean an organization constituted by sovereign States of a given region, to which its member States have transferred competence in respect of matters governed by the present Convention."

[38] Ibid., Art. 42.

[39] See Council of the European Union, Council Decision 2010/48/EC of 26 November 2009 concerning the conclusion, by the European Community, of the United Nations Convention on the Rights of Persons with Disabilities. In Official Journal of the European Union (2010) L 23, p. 35.

[40] See, e.g., CJEU (First Chamber), *DW v Nobel Plastiques Ibérica SA* (Case C-397/18), Judgment, 11 September 2019.

[41] Council of the European Union, Council Directive 2009/13/EC of 16 February 2009 implementing the Agreement concluded by the European Community Shipowners' Associations (ECSA) and

Labour Convention into Union law. As a matter of fact, EU representatives were actively involved in the preparation of the Maritime Labour Convention. Following adoption of the Convention by the International Labour Conference, the EU Council then authorised the Member States to ratify the Maritime Labour Convention. This authorisation was necessary internally, as areas that are regulated by the Convention fall within the exclusive competence of the Union, thus giving the EU exclusive external competence. Almost identical to incorporation of the Maritime Labour Convention into Directive 2009/13/EC is the incorporation of important provisions of Convention No. 188 on work in the fisheries sector into Directive 2017/159/EU. Convention 188 was adopted by the International Labour Conference in 2007. Despite the low level of ratification by EU Member States at the time, in 2012 the relevant social partners reached agreement to incorporate Convention 188 into Union law.[42] The agreement is largely identical in wording to the Convention and was incorporated into Directive 2017/159/EU. The Directive entered into force at the same time as Convention No. 188, on 16 November 2017. It is also welcome, by the way, that the European Commission recently encouraged Member States to ratify the Violence and Harassment Convention, 2019 (No. 190) of the ILO.[43]

An examination of the relationship between the ILO and the EU would be incomplete, however, if one did not also say a word about the significance of ILO standards in the area of the EU customs system. This leads us to the so-called Generalised System of Preferences of the European Union, which grants special tariff advantages to developing countries. According to this system, developing countries receive simplified access to the European market from the EU (so-called "standard GSP"), while the least developed countries are in principle completely free to import into the EU the so-called EBA, the acronym standing for "Everything But Arms", the special arrangement for least developed countries, providing them with duty-free, quota-free access for all products except arms and ammunition. Countries in the GSP category can be granted additional trade benefits provided they comply with certain special arrangements for sustainable development and good governance (so-called "GSP+"). In any case, access to the EU market is conditional on compliance with the eight Conventions that specify the ILO core labour standards. For example, a country wishing to obtain additional benefits under the GSP+ system must ratify and comply with the eight Conventions.[44] In the event of "serious

---

the European Transport Workers' Federation (ETF) on the Maritime Labour Convention, 2006, and amending Directive 1999/63/EC. In Official Journal of the European Union (2009) L124, p. 30.

[42] Council of the European Union, Council Directive (EU) 2017/159 of 19 December 2016 implementing the Agreement concerning the implementation of the Work in Fishing Convention, 2007 of the International Labour Organisation, concluded on 21 May 2012 between the General Confederation of Agricultural Cooperatives in the European Union (Cogeca), the European Transport Workers' Federation (ETF) and the Association of National Organisations of Fishing Enterprises in the European Union (Europêche). In Official Journal of the European Union (2017) L25, p. 12.

[43] European Commission (2020).

[44] See Annex VIII of Reg. (EU) No 978/2012 of the European Parliament and of the Council of 25 October 2012 applying a scheme of generalised tariff preferences and repealing Council Regulation

breaches in the effective application" of the Conventions, the Commission may temporarily withdraw GSP+ status.[45] In all other cases, the conventions do not need to be ratified. However, should "serious and systematic breaches of principles" of the Conventions be identified, these preferences may also be temporarily suspended.[46] Compliance with the agreements is monitored by the Commission. In accordance with the explicit provisions of Regulation 978/2012, the Commission should in particular also take into account the conclusions of the ILO committees.

On paper, this system seems highly convincing. However, there are doubts as to its practical effectiveness in light of the fact that so far none of the beneficiary countries seems to have lost their GSP+ status due to violations of the CLS conventions or other human rights conventions.[47] However, there is also another cause for concern: while the Commission has dealt in detail with assessments of the ILO supervisory organs in the past, the current report, for the years 2016 and 2017, disturbingly no longer refers to the conclusions of the ILO committees to the same extent. And while the country-specific reports for 2016 and 2017 provide a precise account of the latest observations and direct requests by the CEACR that exist for each of the countries, the Commission does not take into account that in both 2016 and 2017 one GSP+ beneficiary country was included in the list of the most serious violations of conventions by the CAS.

3.3 *Privatisation*

If one considers the monitoring and enforcement of international standards, one cannot avoid a phenomenon that is often described as privatisation.[48] The numerous codes of conduct and labels relating to good working conditions are particularly relevant in this context. Privatisation is now so significant that some people are already claiming that a "consumocratic labor law" has emerged. Dumas described this as follows:

(EC) No 732/2008.

[45] See Art. 9(1) of Reg. (EU) No 978/2012 of the European Parliament and of the Council of 25 October 2012 applying a scheme of generalised tariff preferences and repealing Council Regulation (EC) No 732/2008: "A GSP beneficiary country may benefit from the tariff preferences provided under the special incentive arrangement for sustainable development and good governance [...] (b) if it has ratified all the conventions listed in Annex VIII (the 'relevant conventions') and the most recent available conclusions of the monitoring bodies under those conventions (the 'relevant monitoring bodies') do not identify a serious failure to effectively implement any of those conventions [...]."

[46] See Ibid.: "The preferential arrangements referred to in Article 1(2) may be withdrawn temporarily, in respect of all or of certain products originating in a beneficiary country, for any of the following reasons (a) serious and systematic violation of principles laid down in the conventions listed in Part A of Annex VIII [...]."

[47] See for more details Stolzenberg (2019), p. 207.

[48] Cf. Diller (2015), p. 329.

> It is called to supplement protective state law when the latter is inappropriately enforced, but also when inappropriately designed, whether the state is incapable or simply unwilling to protect these populations more efficiently. Under a traditional approach to corporate governance, corporations are indeed free to engage in any kind of profitable activity, provided that they do so in accordance with applicable state laws – even if such activity is known to be socially or environmentally harmful by large segments of the citizenry. To an appreciable extent, the resulting detrimental effects are justified by the inaction of more or less representative states. Consumer regulatory power can be seen in this regard as a serious challenge to a deficient though enduring ideology, one under which it is assumed that the failure by the state to correct common market failures leads to undesirable results deemed (wrongly) to be inevitable.[49]

To be honest, I find the concept interesting, but I do not see "consumocratic law", if there is such a thing, as a fully-fledged substitute for robust international standards.

Privatisation of international standards is in any event often also based on the ILO itself. There are now a number of new models of cooperation between the ILO and governments, workers' representatives and industry representatives in which both national and transnational actors work together. One example is the textile and clothing sector, where a number of projects are now aimed at protecting workers interests: The Better Work program is based on a partnership between the ILO and the International Finance Corporation, a member of the World Bank Group. Under that program, buyers in the apparel industry sign up to ILO-monitored inspections of their factories, and agree to public reporting of results. Better Work is governed at international level by a Management Group comprised of ILO and IFC officials, and is guided by an Advisory Committee of representatives of donor governments, international employers and workers organisations, buyers and independent experts.[50]

Another example is the Accord on Fire and Building Safety in Bangladesh. This agreement was signed in 2013 in the aftermath of the Rana Plaza building collapse that led to the death of more than 1100 people and injured more than 2000. In 2017 a further agreement was concluded, which builds on the previous one.[51] The agreement consists of six key components: A five-year legally binding agreement between brands and trade unions to ensure a safe working environment in the Bangladeshi ready-made garment industry; an independent inspection program; public disclosure of all factories, inspection reports and corrective action plans; a commitment by signatory brands to ensure sufficient funds are available for remediation and to maintain sourcing relationships; establishment of health and safety committees in all factories; worker empowerment through an extensive training program; a complaints mechanism; and the right to refuse unsafe work. The Accord is governed by a Steering Committee with equal representation from trade unions and companies.

[49] Dumas (2013), pp. 67–73. See also Dumas (2015), p. 374.

[50] See the Accord on Fire and Building Safety in Bangladesh, 2013. Available at: https://admin.bangladeshaccord.org/wp-content/uploads/2018/08/2013-Accord.pdf. Accessed 25 Mar 2020.

[51] See the Accord on Fire and Building Safety in Bangladesh, 2018. Available at: https://admin.bangladeshaccord.org/wp-content/uploads/2018/08/2018-Accord.pdf. Accessed 25 Mar 2020.

The ILO serves as a neutral chair.[52] An NGO set up by the Accord parties oversees an inspection system financed by the signatory companies. The Government and local industry, though not parties to the agreement, are to be consulted in administration and management of the program. While the Government's inspection standards apply in principle, the ILO helps to coordinate their application in practice among the actors involved and advises on relevant international labour standards.

Privatisation can also be observed in other ways. For instance, the ILO participates in activities to develop private transnational regulatory instruments. The International Organization for Standardization (ISO), which is increasingly developing voluntary standards in areas of social and public order, deserves particular mention in this respect. However, this is a double-edged sword. Since these standards frequently address issues that are also the subject of international labour standards, there is an increasing need to ensure that such initiatives do not conflict with the provisions of the ILS. Without fundamental coordination, the resulting interplay between industrial standards and national ILS-based labour standards could impair the effectiveness of both systems. On the whole, a final judgement on privatisation still seems too early. For instance, it appears to be very promising in the textile and clothing industry. However, the question arises as to whether the success achieved there can easily be transferred to other areas.

International framework agreements can also play a role in the enforcement of international labour standards. In this respect, one should not be discouraged by the fact that the legally binding effect of such agreements is doubtful, so that it is open whether and to what extent it can be enforced before a court or another dispute settlement institution if necessary. Nor does the lack of a transnational legal framework for the enforcement of such agreements necessarily speak against their effectiveness. This does not mean that framework agreements would be ineffective as such as soft law. At least if embedded in "strong and resilient industrial relations", a framework agreement can certainly develop into a flexible instrument and possibly even encourage the actors to come up with new common solutions.[53] If these conditions are not met, however, there is a real danger that the agreements will remain a "dead letter".

4 Conclusions

To conclude with a few final remarks, I would maintain that monitoring and enforcement of standards within the ILO work quite well. But the system is constantly under scrutiny. And that is a good thing. Closer cooperation between international organisations would be desirable. That way, conflicts could be avoided and

[52] See No. 4 of the Accord on Fire and Building Safety in Bangladesh, 2013. Available at: https://admin.bangladeshaccord.org/wp-content/uploads/2018/08/2013-Accord.pdf. Accessed 25 Mar 2020.

[53] Cf. Krause (2018), pp. 319–334.

synergies could be exploited. A deeper dialogue between all relevant courts and supervisory bodies could contribute to a certain convergence of standards. This would not least be in the interest of those subject to the standards themselves. More could also be done at European Union level to enhance the impact of international standards. The successful cooperation between the ILO and the EU could and should be further intensified. Non-governmental actors—non-governmental organisations, the social partners, consumers—can make a major contribution to the enforcement of international labour standards. The importance of these standards cannot be overestimated. Let us always remember: "In the long run, world peace can only be built on social justice".

References

Beaudonnet X (ed) (2010) International labour law and domestic law: a training manual for judges, lawyers and legal educators. ITC-ILO, Turin

Chen Y (2018) The making of global public authorities: the role of IFIs in setting international labor standards. In: Quayle P, Gao X (eds) AIIB yearbook of international law vol 1: good governance and modern international financial institutions. Brill Nijhoff, Leiden

Committee of Experts on the Application of Conventions and Recommendations (2018) Application of International Labour Standards 2018 – Report III (Part A), International Labour Conference, 107th Session, Geneva, 2018. International Labour Office, Geneva

Diller JM (2015) Pluralism and privatization in transnational labour regulation: experience of the International Labour Organization. In: Blackett A, Trebilcock A (eds) Research handbook on transnational labour law. Edward Elgar, Cheltenham

Dumas PM (2013) Three misunderstandings about consumocratic labor law. Comp Lab Law & Policy J 35(1):67–92

Dumas PM (2015) Thickening soft law through consumocratic law: a pragmatic approach. In: Blackett A, Trebilcock A (eds) Research handbook on transnational labour law. Edward Elgar, Cheltenham

Ebert FC (2015) International financial institutions' approaches to labour law: the case of the International Monetary Fund. In: Blackett A, Trebilcock A (eds) Research handbook on transnational labour law. Edward Elgar, Cheltenham

Ebert FC (2018) Labour standards and the World Bank. Analysing the potential of safeguard policies for protecting workers. In: Gött H (ed) Labour standards in international economic law. Springer, Basel

European Commission (2020) Commission encourages EU Member States to ratify the violence and harassment convention. Available at: https://ec.europa.eu/social/main.jsp?langId=en&catId=89&furtherNews=yes&newsId=9532. Accessed 25 Mar 2020

Humbert F (2018) The WTO and child labour: implications for the debate on international constitutionalism. In: Gött H (ed) Labour standards in international economic law. Springer, Basel

ILO (2018) Freedom of association – compilation of decisions of the committee on freedom of association, 6th edn. International Labour Office, Geneva

ILO (2019a) Handbook of procedures relating to international labour conventions and recommendations (Centenary edition 2019). International Labour Office, Geneva

ILO (2019b) Work for a brighter future – global commission on the future of work. International Labour Office, Geneva

Krause R (2018) The promotion of labour standards through international framework agreements. In: Gött H (ed) Labour standards in international economic law. Springer, Basel

OECD (2011) OECD guidelines for multinational enterprises. OECD Publishing, Paris

Schlachter M (2019) Rezeption des Arbeitsvölkerrechts im Rahmen der ESC. In: Schlachter M, Heuschmid J, Ulber D (eds) Arbeitsvölkerrecht. Mohr Siebeck, Tübingen
Stoll PT (2018) International economic and social dimensions: divided or connected? In: Gött H (ed) Labour standards in international economic law. Springer, Basel
Stolzenberg H (2019) Inspection of the inspectors: is the European Commission sufficiently prosecuting violations of ILO conventions under the GSP regulation? Archiv des Völkerrechts 57(2):207–233
Teklè T (2018) Labour rights and the case law of the European Court of Justice: what role for international labour standards? Eur Lab Law J 9(3):236–262
Thouvenin JM (2015) Diffusion and leveraging of transnational labour norms by the OECD. In: Blackett A, Trebilcock A (eds) Research handbook on transnational labour law. Edward Elgar, Cheltenham
Waas B (2019) Die Normüberwachung durch den ILO-Sachverständigenausschuss für die Durchführung der Übereinkommen und Empfehlungen. Archiv des Völkerrechts 57(2):123–152

Bernd Waas is Full Professor of Labour Law and Civil Law at the Goethe University, Frankfurt am Main. He is a Member of the Committee of Experts on the Application of Conventions and Recommendations (CEACR) of the ILO. He is Coordinator both of the European centre of expertise in the field of labour law, employment and labour market policies (ECE) which assists the Directorate-General for Employment, Social Affairs and Inclusion of the European Commission, and of the European Labour Law Network (ELLN). Moreover, he is Chairman of the German chapter of the International Society for Labour and Social Security Law and a member of the advisory board of the Labour Law Research Network.

Proliferation of Transnational Labour Standards: The Role of the ILO

Yifeng Chen

Contents

1 Introduction

What marks the international labour protection of the past two decades has been the upsurge of transnational labour standards outside the formal scheme of the ILO. Labour standards are increasingly to be found in free trade agreements, investment arrangements, policy documents of international financial institutions (IFIs), and social missions of multinational corporations. Recognizably, a growing body of labour standards has been nested into transnational settings such as the human rights regimes, trade or investment agreements, development finance, or corporate social responsibility.[1] The promotion of labour standards has suddenly become a fashionable cause to pursue. Like it or not, mushrooming transnational labour standards leads to fragmentation, conflicts and competition, both normative and institutional.

While remaining the intellectual centre and normative champion for international labour protection, the ILO no longer enjoys a monopolistic position. As the leading institution in setting and promoting international labour standards, the ILO with its law-making activities has been long appreciated by states, trade unions and other international organizations. However, the making of labour standards has become decentralized. The ILO itself has slowed down its pace of producing

[1] See generally Hepple (2005) and Craig and Lynk (2006).

Y. Chen (✉)
Peking University Law School, Beijing, China
e-mail: yifeng.chen@pku.edu.cn

T. Halonen, U. Liukkunen (eds.), *International Labour Organization and Global Social Governance*, https://doi.org/10.1007/978-3-030-55400-2_5

international labour conventions in recent years. This is in sharp contrast to the proliferation of labour standards outside the ILO. Along with the diffusion of transnational labour standards comes the issue of fragmentation of normativity. The ILO's standards, however authoritative, are not necessarily superior to those formulated in transnational settings. This is aptly described as "competition between mandates and objectives".[2]

In the post-national constellation, labour protection has been mainstreamed as a powerful language for governance and distribution, and international actors have strategically presented themselves as actors of labour governance. The enactment and enforcement of those transnational labour standards are largely self-standing. They are useful supplements, as well as strong competitors, to the international labour conventions and to the existing ILO supervisory mechanisms. They open new paths of global labour governance. These new developments have led to the emergence of transnational labour law as a pertinent field of research.[3]

This chapter examines the possible role of the ILO in the face of fragmentation of labour standards. It starts with a historical account of the institutional transformation of the ILO in the aftermath of the Cold War. Section 2 highlights how the proclamation of fundamental labour rights has equipped the ILO with a managerial vocabulary. Then Sect. 3 traces the trajectory of the diffusion of labour standards in transnational settings, notably in trade agreements and international financial policies. Section 4 examines the relationship between transnational labour standards and ILO standards against a background of institutional competition between regulatory authorities. Section 5 further examines how the fragmentation of labour standards may lead to the institutional politics of substantive labour standards. Section 6 concludes with some critical reflection on the possible strategies the ILO might employ to promote greater consistency and coherence of labour standards in globalization.

2 Coining Fundamental Labour Rights: Inventing a Managerial Vocabulary

The ILO had experienced a bitter institutional transformation in a quest for relevance in the post-Cold War world order.[4] Internally, the usefulness of the ILO was put into question by its Western members as well as the employers' group. Once conceived as an institution of anti-communism,[5] with the collapse of the former

[2] Maupain (2013), p. 18.

[3] See, for example, Blackett and Trebilcock (2015).

[4] Michel Hansenne, who served as Director-General of the ILO from 1989 to 1999, in his several reports to the international labour conference, openly reflected upon various challenges the organization was facing in the post-Cold War era. See, for example, ILO (1994).

[5] This opinion is unambiguously testified by J. Ernest Wilkins, then the Assistant Secretary of Labor for International Labor Affairs with the Eisenhower administration before the Senate of the

Soviet Union the ILO was suddenly seen as being "costly and archaic", and "ill-suited to an era in which the role of labor unions is vastly diminished".[6] The employers' group turned hostile towards the making of international labour standards as well as the operation of ILO supervisory mechanisms.[7] Internationally, the policy-making of economic and financial institutions, taking structural adjustment as an example, was observed to have a larger bearing than the ILO on the conditions of workers.[8] The ILO was simply side-lined in the regulatory vocation of economic globalization.[9] It is useful to recall an internal observation by an ILO official in 1994 that the ILO was facing the challenges of "competing organizations", "competing standards", and ultimately, "competing visions".[10]

Ironically, it was the unresolvable labour/trade debates that reinstated the ILO to the forefront of international policy-making in the mid-1990s. The proposal by the United States at the Uruguay Round to include "internationally recognized labour rights"[11] was strongly resisted by developing countries. Yet the labour/trade debates continued both within and outside the newly established WTO. While the Marrakesh Agreement of 1994 did not include a labour clause, the North American Agreement on Labor Cooperation came into effect on 1 January 1994 as a side deal to the North American Free Trade Agreement. An 1995 OECD study on core workers' rights and international trade suggested that the negative impact of labour rights enforcement on economic competitiveness was unfounded.[12] At the same time, Asian-Pacific countries and developing countries were increasingly concerned over the possibility of labour standards being used for trade protectionist purposes. This led to the decision at the Singapore Ministerial Conference in 1996 to relocate the labour issue back to the ILO. In pronouncing their commitment to "internationally recognized core labour standards", the WTO members expressly acknowledged the ILO as being "the competent body to set and deal with these standards".[13]

United States in 1957. See United States Senate (1957), p. 19.

[6] Quoted from a letter by Jesse Helms, Chairman of the US Senate Foreign Relations Committee sent to Pete V. Domenici, Chairman of the US Senate Budget Committee, dated 26 April 1995. The letter is reproduced in United States Senate (1995), pp. 333–338.

[7] The crisis of tripartism with the ILO continues to this day. See La Hovary (2018).

[8] The ILO tried to initiate institutional dialogue with the World Bank and the IMF as early as the late 1980s. As part of its efforts, the ILO, in cooperation with other parts of the UN system and the Bretton Woods institutions, organized a High-level Meeting on Employment and Structural Adjustment in November 1987, yielding no concrete result.

[9] See ILO (1994), pp. 16–17.

[10] Swepston (1994).

[11] GATT (1987).

[12] OECD (1996).

[13] WTO (1996) Singapore Ministerial Declaration adopted on 13 December 1996, Ministerial Conference, Singapore, 9–13 December 1996. Available at: https://www.wto.org/english/thewto_e/minist_e/min96_e/wtodec_e.htm. Accessed 6 May 2020.

The ILO itself worked proactively to revitalize its institutional role in the face of globalization. As early as June 1994, the Governing Body of the ILO set up the Working Party on the Social Dimensions of the Liberalization of International Trade.[14] The ILO vigilantly followed the involvement of other international organizations in labour issues. In collaborating with the Secretariat of the United Nations, the ILO was substantially involved in preparation for the 1995 World Summit for Social Development. The Copenhagen Declaration and Programme of Action not only affirmed the leading role of the ILO in labour standards, but also for the first time in history formally pronounced the term "basic rights of workers".[15] From the perspective of the ILO, the 1995 World Summit and the 1996 WTO Declaration imbued the ILO with a renewed sense of political meaning and relevance. Seeing the call as an historic opportunity, the then Director-General Michel Hansenne in his 1997 report to the International Labour Conference immediately proposed that the ILO should adopt a declaration pronouncing a list of fundamental labour rights, be selective and strategic in standard-setting, and, most importantly, set the "social rules of the game of globalization".[16]

In 1998 the International Labour Conference had before it the agenda of adopting a declaration on fundamental labour rights. Yet the clash of governmental positions continued from the WTO to the ILO. A Committee on the Declaration of Principles was established by the Conference to reconcile the differences among different groups. The industrialized market economy countries were the active proponents of the declaration. It was asserted that fundamental labour rights were "universal, not relative", "absolute, not conditional", while their promotion constituted "a universal commitment irrespective of the economic, social or cultural conditions of any member State".[17] Moreover, enforcement of those labour standards would not rule out the possibility of recourse to trade measures in addition to the ILO's existing mechanisms.[18] This position was strongly countered by the Asia Pacific Group as well as many developing countries. They were deeply concerned that the WTO might incorporate labour standards and therefore highlighted the ILO as being "the sole competent international organization mandated to set and deal with labour standards". The measures to realize fundamental labour rights should be strictly "promotional and not complaints-based", and not introduce "unilateral or multilateral trade measures".[19]

After lengthy debate, the Declaration on Fundamental Principles and Rights at Work was adopted by the International Labour Conference on 18 June 1998. The Declaration embodies, for the first time in the ILO's history, a set of labour rights

[14] See ILO (1994) Governing Body Working Party on the Social Dimensions of the Liberalization of World Trade (GB.261/WP/SLD/1), Governing Body, 261st Session, Geneva, 1994.

[15] UN (1995).

[16] ILO (1997), p. 26.

[17] As opined by the government member of Canada, see ILO (1998), p. 20/13.

[18] See the opinion of the government member of the United States, ibid., p. 20/108.

[19] See the opinion of the government member of Japan, speaking on behalf of the Asia and Pacific group, ibid., pp. 20/5–6.

characterized by fundamentals, i.e., freedom of association and collective bargaining, prohibition of forced labour, prohibition of child labour, and non-discrimination in respect of employment and occupation.[20] Moreover, the Declaration highlights the universality of fundamental labour rights as they emanate from the ILO constitution. States "have an obligation, arising from the very fact of membership in the Organization, to respect, to promote and to realize" those fundamental principles and rights. It was to the satisfaction of developing countries that the Declaration also states that "labour standards should not be used for protectionist trade purposes".

The Declaration is a self-proclamation of the ILO's constitutional authority on labour regulation in the division of labour among international organizations. By incarnating a set of fundamental labour rights the ILO had successfully reinvigorated its international foothold in globalization.[21] The concept of fundamental labour rights is not primarily addressed to member states, as the Declaration—being "a political statement of a non-binding nature"—does not establish new obligations on ILO members. The genuine audience for the 1998 Declaration, actual or potential, goes beyond ILO constituents, but would reach all relevant international actors such as international trade or financial institutions. The Declaration has enabled the ILO to associate itself with a set of managerial vocabulary, and to have a fair share in regulatory competition in deepening globalization. In this sense, the Declaration is indeed a step towards revitalization, not retreat.[22]

The adoption of the 1998 Declaration also marks a profound institutional transformation of the ILO.[23] Since then, the ILO has reformed its traditional approach to international labour standard-setting. The ILO is no longer obsessed with making hard international labour conventions. The number of labour conventions produced by the ILO has steadily declined over the past two decades. The ILO also increasingly uses declarations, recommendations and other soft documents for its normative activities. In addition to setting standards for states, the ILO increasingly addresses international organizations, social partners and others. The ILO does not only provide the forum for states to debate and formulate labour standards, but has also turned itself into a developmental organization to promote labour standards.[24] The

---

[20] The core labour rights enshrined in the Declaration are embodied in and endorsed by eight ILO fundamental conventions, chronologically, the Forced Labour Convention, adopted 28 June 1930 (No. 29); the Freedom of Association and Protection of the Right to Organize Convention, adopted 9 July 1948 (No. 87); the Right to Organize and Collective Bargaining Convention, adopted 1 July 1949 (No. 98); the Equal Remuneration Convention, adopted 29 June 1951 (No. 100); the Abolition of Forced Labour Convention, adopted 25 June 1957 (No. 105); the Discrimination (Employment and Occupation) Convention, adopted 25 June 1958 (No. 111); the Minimum Age Convention, adopted 26 June 1973 (No. 138); and the Worst Forms of Child Labour Convention, adopted 17 June 1999 (No. 182).

[21] See de Wet (2010).

[22] See Maupain (2005).

[23] For a useful account of the origin, history and reality of the 1998 Declaration from an insider's perspective, see Tapiola (2018).

[24] See Standing (2008).

ILO has transformed from a relatively closed inter-state institution to a dynamic global actor.

With the adoption of the 1998 Declaration and its follow-up, the ILO embarked upon fundamental labour rights advocacy. This includes two strategies. One front is the campaign with the member states for universal ratification of ILO fundamental labour conventions, a recognizable success if measured by the growth in the number of treaty ratifications. On the other front, the ILO has initiated dialogues on the possible integration of labour standards with international organizations whose work may have significant labour ramifications, including international financial institutions. A growing international recognition of fundamental labour rights was observed as of the beginning of the new millennium.

Since then, the leading role of the ILO in labour issues receives broad recognition from other international organizations. In 2008 the ILO further adopted its Declaration on Social Justice for a Fair Globalization, asserting the ILO's "responsibility to examine and consider all international economic and financial policies in the light of the fundamental objective of social justice".[25] Inter-agency cooperation between the ILO and international financial institutions, despite their continued differences in terms of approaches to labour, was further deepened after the 2008 economic crisis.[26]

3 The Proliferation of Labour Standards: The Rise of Transnationalism

As the ILO endeavoured to reinvigorate its role in international labour regulation, an observable trend has been the global diffusion of labour standards in transnational settings. Indeed, the recognition and enforcement of labour standards in transnational settings can hardly find its role in the traditional procedures of ILO standard-setting practice. The process started with the signing of the North American Agreement on Labor Cooperation by Canada, the United States, and Mexico on 14 September 1993.[27] While the level of protection defers largely to national labour law and cooperation was provided for exchanges of information, technical assistance and consultations, the Agreement nevertheless established a dispute settlement procedure for dealing with "persistent patterns of failure" to effectively enforce technical labour standards on occupational safety and health, child labour and minimum

[25] ILO, Declaration on Social Justice for a Fair Globalization. Adopted by the International Labour Conference, 97th Session, Geneva, 10 June 2008.

[26] The Summit of G20 at London in April 2009 requested the ILO to assess the labour impact of the actions taken and advise on further measures. See G20 Leaders' Statement, The Global Plan for Recovery and Reform, 2 April 2009. Available at: https://www.treasury.gov/resource-center/international/g7-g20/Documents/London%20April%202009%20Leaders%20final-communique.pdf. Accessed 6 May 2020.

[27] For an early account, see Compa (1995).

wage.[28] Backed by the possibility of trade sanctions, a third-party mechanism as such was not only progressive and innovative, but also seen by many as aggressive and intrusive.

The second treaty of the United States that referred to labour waited until its free trade agreement (FTA) with Jordan in 2000. The labour chapter of this FTA is succinct. It made express reference to the commitment of the parties to the 1998 ILO Declaration. In terms of substantive protection, it covers "internationally recognized labor rights" and parties are under a specific obligation not to "encourage trade by relaxing domestic labor laws".[29] As the US Trade Act of 2002 requires the government to pursue promotion and enforcement of international labour rights, almost all subsequent FTAs concluded by the United States incorporate a labour chapter. Examples include the United States-Singapore Free Trade Agreement of 2003, the United States-Central America Free Trade Agreement of 2004, and a number of others. The most ambitious labour chapter was probably the Trans-Pacific Partnership Agreement of 2016 under the Obama administration,[30] although the signature of the United States was shortly withdrawn with the change of administration.

Since 2008, states have been more receptive towards the inclusion of a labour provision in FTAs. The number of FTAs with a labour provision has grown rapidly. According to the ILO, by 2016 there were "a total of 77 trade agreements with labour provisions, involving 136 economies".[31] Notably the United States, Canada, and the European Union have been the most active promoters in this regard. It is also observed by the ILO that the majority of labour provisions are to be found in agreements between developed and developing countries, accounting for 70.1% of the total number of FTAs with a labour provision.[32] Yet most FTAs on labour relates to information, cooperation and technical assistance. The application of dispute settlement procedure to the enforcement of labour standards is still rare, and often only if and to the extent that violation of labour standards has directly affected trade between the parties.[33]

Outside trade agreements, a parallel development has been the changing attitude of IFIs and their growing engagement with labour protection. The incorporation of labour protection into the work of IFIs has been a fairly recent phenomenon. The change of position is largely a response to growing external pressure wrought on

[28] Canada-Mexico-United States: North American Agreement on Labor Cooperation. In: American Society of International Law (1993) International Legal Materials 32(6): 1499–1518.

[29] United States (U.S.)-Jordan: Agreement Between The United States of America and the Hashemite Kingdom of Jordan on the Establishment of a Free Trade Area. In: American Society of International Law (2002) International Legal Materials 41(1): pp. 63–85.

[30] Trans-Pacific Partnership Agreement, 4 February 2016.

[31] International Labour Office (2016) Third Item on the Agenda – labour-related provisions in trade agreements: recent trends and relevance to the ILO (GB.328/POL/3), Governing Body, 328th Session, Geneva, 27 October–10 November 2016.

[32] ILO (2017), p. 12.

[33] See Bolle (2016).

IFIs. The neo-liberal prescriptions of IFIs met with doubts from borrowing countries and were increasingly challenged among scholars in 2000s. Pressure from the trade unions in large shareholders, such as the American Federation of Labor and Congress of Industrial Organization (AFL–CIO),[34] also plays an influential role in pressing for the policy changes of the World Bank and the International Monetary Fund (IMF).

Labour protection started to enter into the work of IFIs only after the 2000s. This was pioneered by a modest reference to core labour standards in the social protection strategy of the Asian Development Bank (ADB) in 2001. The ADB committed to ensuring that its procurement of goods and services, contractors, subcontractors and consultants would be in compliance with core labour standards.[35] Full recognition of labour standards had to wait until the adoption of Performance Standards on Social and Environmental Sustainability by the International Finance Corporation (IFC) in 2006.[36] Labour and working conditions are featured as a self-standing performance standard under the IFC. This was the first time a significant IFI had given its full endorsement to labour standards in an operational policy.

The successful incorporation of labour standards by the IFC is largely attributable to the fact that the IFC engages exclusively in private sectors. Those potential clients who gain access to the IFC are usually economically better-off, administratively well-organized companies. These IFC policy requirements are often in alignment with existing corporate policies on social responsibility and their implementation does not raise insurmountable difficulties from the perspective of a company. Moreover, in essence, the labour policy of the IFC usually goes little beyond requiring companies to comply with existing national laws where they operate. The scenario would get much more complicated if an IFI which engages principally in public lending tries to extend its policy to labour issues.

The example set by the IFC was quickly followed by the European Bank for Reconstruction and Development (EBRD) in 2008.[37] The EBRD adopted its first environmental policy in 1991.[38] A renewed version of the Environmental and Social Policy was adopted in 2008, with labour and working conditions inserted as a separate standard.[39] The EBRD acknowledges its due diligence obligation not to finance projects in contravention of the host country's international legal obligations on environmental protection and human rights. At the same time, the European Investment Bank (EIB) in 2009 adopted Environmental and Social Principles and

[34] The AFL–CIO has repeatedly requested the World Bank and IMF to commit to international labour standards. See, for example, AFL–CIO (1998); AFL–CIO (2000).

[35] ADB (2003), pp. 15–16.

[36] IFC (2006).

[37] The EBRD expressly acknowledged that its policy review is partly driven by the adoption of performance standards by the IFC in 2006. See EBRD (2008a), p. 42.

[38] It is to be noticed that in the previous version of the Environmental Policy of 2003, the EBRD had already addressed "worker protection issues" including occupational health and safety, harmful child labour, forced labour and discriminatory practices. See EBRD (2003).

[39] EBRD (2008b).

Standards and expressly acknowledged ILO core labour standards.[40] The EIB policy applies to both public and private sectors, albeit the ensuing obligations of clients in different sectors do differ in nature.[41]

The precedents set by the IFC, the EBRD and the EIB were inspiring and encouraged other IFIs. Since then, there has been a growing acceptance of labour standards among IFIs. Of course, a number of IFIs have refrained from instituting a labour policy so far—the IMF and the International Fund for Agricultural Development (IFAD) being prominent examples. As for those IFIs that incorporate labour standards, there are roughly two categories. In some cases, a comprehensive framework for labour protection has been pursued. For example, in 2013 the African Development Bank (AfDB) Group[42] adopted its Integrated Safeguards System.[43] Its policy on labour protection is also comprehensive and is close to that of the IFC and of the EBRD. Another high profile case was the adoption by the World Bank of its Environmental and Social Framework in 2016 after several years of consultation and debates. In those cases, labour protection is established as a highly elaborate, substantive, and self-standing standard.

In some other cases, a succinct version of an environmental and social policy is enacted with a brief reference to labour standards. An example here might be the Sustainability Policy of the Nordic Investment Bank (NIB) adopted on 1 September 2011, with the NIB requiring its clients to respect the four core labour rights and to provide safe and healthy working conditions.[44] The Black Sea Trade and Development Bank (BSTDB) also upgraded its Environmental and Social Policy in 2013 and openly committed to "respect for human rights in a working environment", as embodied in ILO core labour standards.[45] In 2016 the New Development Bank (NDB) adopted its Environmental and Social Framework which sets occupational health and safety at the centre of labour protection.[46] And in the same year, the Asian Infrastructure Investment Bank (AIIB) approved its Environmental and Social Framework and prescribed labour standards for both public and private sectors. In addition, projects involving use of forced labour or child labour are expressly listed on the AIIB's list of exclusions from financing.[47]

It is safe to summarize that the development of international labour protection during recent decades is characterized by the proliferation of labour standards in transnational settings. The body of transnational labour standards is not monolithic, but rather amorphous. It is not a single set of uniform labour standards, but an

[40] EIB (2013), pp. 18–19.

[41] Ibid, p. 15.

[42] The African Development Bank Group includes the African Development Bank (AfDB) and African Development Fund (AfDF).

[43] African Development Bank Group (2013).

[44] NIB (2012).

[45] See BSTDB (2014).

[46] NDB (2016).

[47] AIIB (2016).

aggregation of various sets of independent labour standards practised in transnational settings. To group all those standards under the label of transnational labour standards risks reduction and oversimplification of the richness, diversity and nuances of labour standards in transnational settings. Yet, they share the sentiment that labour standards may grow and develop outside the ILO conventions, and may not rely on the ILO for their implementation.

One should not overlook the heterogeneity and richness of those transnational labour standards. Yet, some core elements may be observed. Firstly, the ILO conventions and standards, prominently the 1998 Declaration, have been the centrepiece of the normative project of transnational labour standards. Most of them have made express reference to the 1998 Declaration.[48] In most cases, all four categories of fundamental labour rights are acknowledged. Yet, it is still not very clear from a normative perspective whether this reference would endow those fundamental labour rights with an additional layer of normativity. It is also interesting to observe that the substantive labour rights covered by the FTAs and IFIs are in growing convergence.

Secondly, those transnational labour standards usually go beyond the purview of fundamental labour rights. Typically, these may involve safe working conditions. This is the least politically sensitive and morally uncontested part of labour standards. It is among the first cluster of labour standards received by the IFIs. The World Bank's current standards on occupational health and safety are extensive. They require, among others things, identification of potential hazards, preventive and protective measures, preparedness for and responses to emergencies, and effective remedies for occupational injuries, deaths, disability and disease. Other standards may involve workers' rights related to hours of work, minimum wages, overtime compensation and benefits,[49] social security,[50] and the protection of migrant workers.[51]

Thirdly, these transnational labour standards are designed with autonomous mechanisms of enforcement. In the case of FTAs, labour standards are enforceable through cooperation, technical assistance and labour consultation, or even by recourse to dispute settlement procedures or unilateral trade sanctions. In 2014 the United States brought the first labour dispute case against Guatemala, utilizing the dispute settlement procedure under the Dominican Republic-Central America-United States Free Trade Agreement, yet failed to establish the failure of Guatemala's enforcement of its labour law in a sustained or recurring manner according to the

[48] International Labour Office (2016) Third Item on the Agenda – labour-related provisions in trade agreements: recent trends and relevance to the ILO (GB.328/POL/3), Governing Body, 328th Session, Geneva, 27 October–10 November 2016; Agustí-Panareda et al. (2014).

[49] International Labour Office (2016) Third Item on the Agenda – labour-related provisions in trade agreements: recent trends and relevance to the ILO (GB.328/POL/3), Governing Body, 328th Session, Geneva, 27 October–10 November 2016, p. 54.

[50] See EBRD (2008b).

[51] See EIB (2013), p. 70.

final report of the arbitration panel in 2017.[52] In the case of IFIs, labour standards are enforceable through a variety of means and procedures, including prior plans or commitments of the borrower, a project-specific on-site grievance mechanism, independent labour inspection, or an IFI complaint mechanism. This means that these transnational labour standards are not only independent from the ILO, but also may be more effective than ILO supervisory mechanisms.

In the course of diffusion of labour standards, the ILO has played an indispensable role. It has been not unusual that the ILO gets involved or is consulted in the labour provisions of FTAs. The ILO itself has confirmed that "trade partners have requested the ILO's advice through technical assistance on various questions related to labour standards and practices".[53] This applies even more so in the case of IFI labour standards. For example, the EBRD actively resorted to ILO expertise when designing its labour standards. In 2006, a thematic meeting on labour issues was hosted by the ILO where EBRD staff met with representatives from trade unions, employers, and ILO experts.[54] Another prominent example can be found in the formulation of the Environmental and Social Framework of the World Bank. The World Bank has organized three labour expert meetings respectively in Jakarta (2013), London (2015) and Washington (2015).[55] In all these meetings, ILO representatives were present.

Inter-agency learning is also an important factor accounting for the spread of labour standards in the case of IFIs. The Multilateral Finance Institutions Working Group on the Environment (MFI-WGE) was initiated in the 1990s and serves as a useful platform for senior IFI managers to discuss and coordinate policies towards environmental and social issues. As social issues are increasingly included in safeguards policy, this working group was recently renamed as the Multilateral Finance Institutions Working Group on Environmental and Social Standards (MFI-WGESS). This working group is rather informal but has been instrumental for institutional learning on environmental and social standards. For example, the African Development Bank expressly acknowledged that its earlier drafts of safeguards policies "have been reviewed by the IFC, World Bank, Asian Development Bank and other members of the MFI Working Group on the Environment (MFI-WGE)".[56] The World Bank also expressly acknowledged that its labour standards are "derived from provisions of other MDBs [multilateral development banks]".[57]

---

[52] Arbitral Panel established pursuant to Chapter 20 of the CAFTA-DR (2017).

[53] International Labour Office (2016) Third Item on the Agenda – labour-related provisions in trade agreements: recent trends and relevance to the ILO (GB.328/POL/3), Governing Body, 328th Session, Geneva, 27 October–10 November 2016.

[54] See EBRD (2006), p. 11.

[55] See World Bank (2013, 2015a, b).

[56] See the statement in African Development Bank Group (2013), Acknowledgements.

[57] World Bank (2014a), p. 11.

4 In Relation to ILO Standards: The Ambivalence of Transnational Labour Standards

An interesting aspect of transnational labour standards is their relationship with ILO standards. More specifically, when transnational labour standards give concrete expressions to core labour standards, should reference be to the ILO fundamental labour conventions and the ILO Declaration on Fundamental Principles and Rights at Work of 1998, or should transnational labour standards simply embody the substance of the core labour standards without resorting or referring to specific ILO documents?

The practice has been diverse. Some IFIs tend to make a full reference to the ILO fundamental labour conventions. This is the case for the IFC's Performance Standards of 2006. The IFC expressly acknowledges that its labour standards "have been in part guided by a number of international conventions negotiated through the ILO and the UN". A further reference to all eight ILO fundamental labour conventions was detailed in a footnote.[58] The same applies more or less to the EBRD's Environmental and Social Policy of 2008, and to the AfDB Group's Integrated Safeguards System of 2013. Some other IFIs with a relevant succinct policy document may avoid explicit reference to the ILO conventions, as in the case of the NIB's Sustainability Guidelines of 2012. Another way of looking at the matter is by examining the portfolios and activities of the IFIs. Those IFIs engaged more, or exclusively, with the private sector are more inclined to refer to the ILO conventions. On the contrary, those engaged more with the public sector are more cautious in referring to the ILO conventions.

It seems that FTAs are more receptive towards referring to the ILO Declaration and fundamental labour rights. Most recent FTAs with labour provisions have made reference to the 1998 Declaration. It has been customary for Canada to refer to the 1998 Declaration in its FTAs with labour provision. Yet, the degree of integration varies under different FTAs, as do the legal effects of the ILO Declaration.[59] For example, the North American Free Trade Agreement of 2018 makes repeated reference to the 1998 Declaration.[60] In the EU-Canada Comprehensive Economic and Trade Agreement of 2016, the agreement actually calls upon the states to "make continued and sustained efforts to ratify the fundamental ILO Conventions if they have not yet done so".[61]

To refer or not to refer to ILO standards is not just a matter of formality or theoretical interest. Rather, this will largely affect the normative operation of transnational labour standards, as well as their foundational authority. Are transnational labour standards simply to be understood as no more than a transposed expression of established ILO labour standards, or rather, does their authority derive from the

[58] IFC (2012), Performance Standard 2 Labor and Working Conditions, para 2.

[59] Agustí-Panareda et al. (2014).

[60] North American Free Trade Agreement, 30 November 2018.

[61] EU-Canada Comprehensive Economic and Trade Agreement, 30 October 2016.

labour provisions themselves and as such constitute a set of labour standards *sui generis*? And if there should arise differences of opinion on certain labour standards, would the IFIs or trade partners have to resort to the ILO conventions and relevant jurisprudence to search for a correct interpretation, or would the IFIs or trade partners be entitled to develop their own institutional standards and jurisprudence?

When the World Bank drafted its labour standards, a number of Western countries requested the World Bank to link its labour standards to the ILO conventions.[62] The United States urged the Bank to incorporate reference to the ILO Declaration on the Fundamental Principles and Rights at Work.[63] The ILO also actively lobbied for the inclusion of the ILO conventions. An obvious advantage of reference to the ILO conventions is that the very content of IFI labour standards has a reliable source and solid ground. To borrow the ILO standards could avoid re-opening many debates that were already concluded at the time of drafting ILO conventions. At the end of the day, since IFIs are not specialized in labour protection, it may be desirable to heed the knowledge and expertise of the ILO. Moreover, as the ILO standards are internationally recognized, it may also be conducive to a uniform application of labour standards.

Yet, the proposal to incorporate the ILO conventions in World Bank social policies was viewed with much vigilance among developing countries. The major concern is that this might amount to a *de facto* imposition of the ILO conventions and bypass ratification procedures.[64] In other words, the ILO fundamental labour conventions may be enforced through World Bank policies against a borrowing country even if the country has not acceded to all the ILO fundamental conventions. The traditional ILO approach to the promotion of labour standards relies upon voluntary ratification of labour conventions by states. And to ratify, or not to ratify, a treaty is always an essential feature of the sovereign prerogative. However, if the ILO conventions are referred to in the labour standards of the IFIs, then sovereign borrowers are obliged to implement those labour standards in the role of clients irrespective of their non-ratification. World Bank labour standards would be equivalent to a coerced application of the ILO conventions. It is therefore in the consultation phase that China suggested the Bank confine itself to reference to general principles, but not to the ILO conventions.[65]

At the same time, there is another important aspect to the matter. It would not only have normative relevance on the operation of transnational labour standards, but also has strong implications for the relationship between international actors and the ILO. It is in the interest of the ILO to develop a body of ILO-centred labour

[62] See for an example, World Bank (2014b).

[63] World Bank (2015c).

[64] For example, the ADB considers the core labour standards as automatically applicable. "Internationally recognized labor standards, when ratified, are also part of the legislative framework of a DMC. With regard to the Core Labor Standards, no explicit ratification is needed for them to be part of the legislative framework of a country." See ADB (2003), p. 15.

[65] World Bank (2015d).

standards at the global level. A reference to the ILO and its work would naturally reinforce the authority of the ILO in labour matters. To a certain extent, a strengthened role for the ILO is also in the interest of the international community in general. The emergence of autonomous labour standards outside the ILO system could possibly divert and compete with the ILO and its standard-setting authority.

Seen in this light, one may gain a better appreciation of the institutional rivalry between the World Bank and the ILO. The World Bank in its Environmental and Social Framework decided against direct reference to any ILO instruments.[66] In explaining its decision, the World Bank made it very clear that it is exactly the autonomy of labour standards and of the Bank that animates such a political decision:

> It is Management's view that the requirement for both World Bank and Borrower to comply with the ES [Environmental and Social] Framework should be self-standing, and should not require reference to external sources to make this judgment.[67]

The ILO was profoundly disappointed at this decision. Immediately after the World Bank published its Environmental and Social Framework, the ILO publicly pronounced its dissatisfaction. It stated that "from the outset the ILO expressed concern with Bank Management's decision to exclude direct references to ILO core labour conventions from the ESF [Environmental and Social Framework]."[68]

The case of the World Bank makes a good example that highlights the autonomous status of transnational labour standards. The legal validity of these labour standards does not depend on the ILO conventions or other normative documents. Nor is the substance of those transnational labour standards defined or constrained by the ILO conventions. Transnational labour standards constitute a set of independent, self-contained labour standards with distinct sources, procedures and mechanisms, in parallel to the traditional concept of international labour law centred on and formulated by the ILO. Although these labour standards do strengthen labour protection at global and transnational levels, they are necessarily associated with the ILO standards. In this sense, even though the substance of transnational labour standards might be identical to those in ILO standards, they are capable of supplementing, or even competing with, ILO standards. They are not at all simply a repetition of existing standards.

The difference between the World Bank and the ILO is not concerned with actual labour standards, but about who is entitled to prescribe labour protection in an increasingly globalized world. While the authority of the ILO is highly acknowledged, the World Bank has refused to concede the ILO a monopolized say on labour standards. Putting it differently, the ILO does not have higher authority than the World Bank in speaking to labour standards. It can be expected that close

[66] The attitude of the World Bank towards external institutions has been consistently conservative. A known example is World Bank's explicit rejection of the binding force of the resolution of the United Nations (UN) Security Council acting under the Chapter VII of the UN Charter.

[67] World Bank (2015e).

[68] ILO (2016).

cooperation between the World Bank and the ILO will increase and grow steadily in the future. Meanwhile, with assistance from the ILO, the World Bank is likely to develop its own expertise and knowledge in labour protection in connection with its own labour policy and project implementation.

5 Institutional Politics of Labour Standards

Even though core labour standards receive broad endorsement, their substance and actual enforcement exhibit profound differences in practice. For example, it is noticed that different countries have very different approaches to the workers' right of unionization. There was, and probably still is, hesitation among IFIs to include freedom of association and collective bargaining, which is considered a highly political and sensitive issue in borrowing countries. Even for those rights of a seemingly less political nature, such as the prohibition of child labour, the matter may also be received with divergent attitudes in different cultures.

Freedom of association is probably the most politically sensitive right of workers. For many countries, freedom of association lies at the heart of labour protection. And freedom of association is deeply embedded in the liberal political tradition. Labour protection through institutionalized unionization of labour has functioned in a highly effective manner in countries like Sweden and Finland.[69] Yet in some other countries the right to organize is not purely a matter of labour protection and its exercise is restricted by law or in practice.[70] This may include prior approval or registration of the formation of trade unions, and other forms of restriction. The difference of positions among states towards the right to organize is also demonstrated by the fact that a number of countries have not ratified the Freedom of Association and Protection of the Right to Organize Convention (No. 87) or the Right to Organize and Collective Bargaining Convention (No. 98). Out of the eight ILO fundamental conventions, these two conventions have received the least number of ratifications.[71]

The initial attitude of IFIs towards freedom of association has also been deeply cautious. The labour rights tackled by IFIs used to have a limited spectrum with a special focus on safe working conditions and prohibition of child or forced labour. An explicit reference to freedom of association was often absent. As observed by

[69] See for example Fahlbeck and Mulder (2009), pp. 16–18.

[70] See the observations of the ILO in its global report on the freedom of association, in ILO (2008), p. 11.

[71] By the end of May 2020, 155 countries had ratified the ILO Convention No. 87. See ILO (n.d.-a). 167 countries have ratified ILO Convention No. 98. See ILO (n.d.-b). These numbers are much lower than other 6 ILO fundamental conventions. In contrast, the Worst Forms of Child Labour Convention (No. 182) has received 186 ratifications so far.

Francis Maupin, the former legal counsel of the ILO, "freedom of association and collective bargaining continue to be regarded as civil rights which [World] Bank activities might facilitate, but it still believes that it is not in its mandate to actively promote them, and even less so where they might interfere with economic performance".[72] This is partly due to the economic perspective of seeing trade unions negatively as free riders.[73] Moreover, many developing countries where the IFIs operate hold a conservative position towards freedom of association, and those IFIs engaging with public sectors are barred from interfering in the internal affairs of the borrowing sovereigns. This was still the case when the World Bank proposed its first draft of the Environmental and Social Framework in 2014. In its standard on labour and working conditions, the World Bank refrained from mentioning freedom of association among its objectives, instead adopting a deferential attitude to the borrowing country. It expressly limited its support to freedom of association, that is, only if the national laws of the borrowing country recognize it.[74]

This cautious approach by the World Bank met with fierce criticism from labour NGOs and experts, the ILO and developed countries.[75] The main arguments are summarized as follows. To start with, all core labour standards are indivisible and as a whole they constitute the floor of protection for workers. There is no reason to segregate freedom of association from other standards. Secondly, freedom of association and collective bargaining are political rights by nature, as indeed are other core labour standards. Freedom of association cannot justifiably be excluded on the grounds of its political nature. Thirdly, the silence of the World Bank might be construed as being permissive of suppressive or retaliatory measures against workers seeking to exercise freedom of association. Fourthly, the obligation to promote core labour standards arises from states' membership in the ILO. As such, neither the World Bank nor the states themselves should refuse to implement freedom of association on the basis of national laws.[76]

The World Bank quickly yielded to this pressure after the first round of consultation. The Bank switched to the opposite position in the second draft of the Environmental and Social Framework and provided unqualified support to freedom of association as part of its labour policy. This radical change of position generated great concern among developing countries. The primary concern was the unqualified nature of the World Bank statement. It is suggested by countries such as China that the exercise of freedom of association and collective bargaining should be in accordance with the national laws of borrowing countries.[77] Some also suggest that the arrangement concerning freedom of association and collective bargaining should

[72] Maupain (2013), p. 78.

[73] It used to be the mainstream opinion of the World Bank, see Murphy (2014), pp. 405 and 417.

[74] World Bank (2014c).

[75] See World Bank (2015f).

[76] ITUC/Global Unions (2014), pp. 2–3.

[77] For the opinions of China, see World Bank (2015g).

be expressed so as not to frustrate project implementation.[78] In response, the World Bank decided to qualify its wording to "support the principles of freedom of association and collective bargaining of project workers in a manner consistent with national law".[79] This formula entered the final text of the World Bank's Environmental and Social Policy in 2016. Yet, this formula does not satisfy the ILO and trade unions, who see this as a concession from the internationally accepted standards.[80]

One may further suggest that the challenge for IFIs in terms of incorporating labour standards is not only institutional, but also intellectual and philosophical. The most difficult part is how to integrate labour protection into the mainstream economic theories of IFIs. Typically, an economic perspective treats labour as a factor of production and is usually in favour of flexibility of labour markets and deregulation of social protection.

The controversies surrounding the World Bank publication "Doing Business" provide another illustrative example of embedded neoliberal economic thoughts among IFIs.[81] "Doing Business" is a flagship publication of the World Bank, launched in 2004, aiming to measure the business environment across the world with quantitative indicators. In its early years, the "Employing Workers" indicator largely measured rigidity of hiring and firing workers and their employment conditions. Its underpinning philosophy is that rigid labour regulation leads to unemployment in formal sectors, and ultimately reduction in productivity growth.[82] Accordingly, the more regulatory and protective a country's labour regulations are, the lower the ranking it receives.[83] And among the recommended reform measures are introduction of part-time and fixed-term employment contracts, and reduction of the minimum wage for young workers.[84]

This provoked fierce protests from the ILO, trade unions and labour law scholars in general.[85] The ILO criticized the methodological flaws of the Employing Workers indicator and expressed the concern that the ranking system would "discourage countries from ratifying and abiding by international labour Conventions and Recommendations".[86] The international trade unions are profoundly concerned with the fundamental bias against labour regulation of the Employing Workers indicator. They condemned in particular the fact that the World Bank, in using the

[78] World Bank (2016a), p. 4.

[79] World Bank (2016b), p. 22.

[80] The qualification of "in a manner consistent with national law" was harshly criticized by the ILO for the reason that the formula as such "undercuts the universal principles adhered to by the ILO's 187 member states and jeopardizes the purpose of having such an objective". See ILO (2016).

[81] For the ongoing controversy regarding the publication, see Murphy (2014).

[82] See World Bank (2003), p. 29.

[83] On the politics of knowledge behind the ranking and a case study of the Doing Business Indicators, see Davis et al. (2012).

[84] See World Bank (2003), p. 30.

[85] See Kryvoi (2009), pp. 47–59.

[86] See International Labour Office (2007).

indicators, was eliminating workers' protection.[87] In response, the World Bank conceded a more balanced approach to labour protection, committed to a better alignment with ILO core labour standards,[88] and subsequently broadened the spectrum of measurement to include protective elements such as job quality. As of 2011, "Doing Business" has removed labour regulation from the measuring criteria of ranking. Instead, labour regulation is included in the publication only as a referential annex.

Both examples referred to above fully illustrate that labour standards, when transplanted in transnational settings, are constrained and affected by institutional philosophy, culture and norms. Transnational labour standards live different normative lives of their own. They may borrow the ILO standards at their convenience, but are not reluctant to challenge ILO's claim of normative superiority. The politics of labour standards is not only normative and institutional, but also ideological and philosophical.

6 The Future of the ILO: Leadership in Intellectuality and Normativity

When established in 1919, the ILO was undoubtedly the only regulatory authority for labour and social life at that time. Entering into the new millennium, the international regulation of labour has turned out to be a crowded field. In addition to the proliferation of normative standards, there is also competition for regulatory competence, and struggle for institutional ideologies. This generates the risk of legal uncertainty, the possibility of forum shopping, as well as inflation of labour rhetoric.

The proliferation of labour standards does not necessarily by itself promise a world of better labour protection. The actual effect of transnational labour standards usually does not offset the adverse impact caused by international economic arrangements. Labour provisions in FTAs could be incorporated to appease anticipated criticism and used to legitimize FTAs,[89] but may not be able to deliver the aspirations promised on paper. They are even more radically criticised as an instrument of "mutually assured non-compliance".[90] While adoption of the labour standards by the World Bank was applauded, the limited scope of application among other things also raised doubts as to its practical effectiveness.[91] Concern was also expressed that the challenge for IFIs in fully incorporating labour standards are

[87] ITUC/Global Unions (2007).

[88] See World Bank (2009), pp. 22–23; World Bank (2010), p. 94.

[89] See Santos (2019), pp. 140–174.

[90] See Tham and Ewing (2020).

[91] See, for example, Ebert (2018).

philosophical, constitutional and cultural.[92] There is indeed a danger of "economisation of core labour rights".[93]

The foremost challenge ahead for the ILO is less about fragmentation of norms, but more about the philosophy of and approach to labour. The difference between a neoliberal approach and a rights-based approach is indeed structural. Another telling example is the attitude of IFIs towards trade unions. The trade unions are considered to be free riders in the view of the World Bank.[94] The IMF is reported to hold the same opinion.[95] In essence, trade unions are difficult to analyze in economic terms of efficiency and productivity. In the 2017 evaluation of the IMF on its social policy, some IMF staff members were reported to have felt that the IMF and ILO staffs "did not speak the same language".[96]

To fully integrate labour protection in economic globalization would require a profound change in economic thinking to reconceptualize labour protection as an inherent good. Labour should be approached not purely as a factor of production in economic terms, but also as one of the very foundational values upon which economic activities are based. In other words, trade arrangement and financial institutions have to embed labour protection into their economic work from their foundational philosophy, that is to say, what are the elements of a sound economy and where the boundary of economic activities lies.[97] This in practice would mean modifying or even rewriting the philosophy of mainstream economic theory, which is a formidable task, if not an impossible one. It would also require the ILO to engage boldly not just in setting labour standards, but in formulating competing economic and social theories against those currently accepted.

At the technical level, the ILO also bears a special responsibility to promote coherence of and genuine respect for labour standards at the global level. First of all, the ILO may wish to further strengthen its normative grip on fundamental labour rights. What the ILO did in its 1998 Declaration was to emphasize the universality of those rights by linking them to the ILO membership of states. Yet this universal approach has the shortcomings of being soft and vague. It places undue emphasis on principles rather than rights, and is also detached from the international labour conventions.[98] It has been increasingly felt that a reference to the 1998 Declaration does little to clarify the rights as set out in labour provisions.[99] It may be time for the ILO to review its soft law approach and reconsider the possibility of adopting a

[92] See Chen (2018).

[93] See Breining-Kaufmann (2007).

[94] See Murphy (2014), pp. 405 and 417.

[95] See Ebert (2015).

[96] IMF (2017), p. 30.

[97] For example, the integration of environmental protection in the policy of the World Bank is greatly facilitated by the publication of "Development and the Environment" in 1992, which "presented environmental issues in a language that economists (inside and outside the Bank) could understand". See Wade (1997), pp. 712–713.

[98] See Alston (2004).

[99] See, for examples, Ushakova (2018); also Tham and Ewing (2020).

comprehensive fundamental labour rights convention. This convention could be open to states and international organizations alike for accession.

Secondly, at the inter-agency level the ILO might also be more actively engaged in the enforcement of transnational labour standards. Some trade agreements actually conceive such a role for the ILO. For example, the EU-Canada Comprehensive Economic and Trade Agreement stipulates that, when the dispute settlement procedure is resorted to for settling issues related to fundamental labour rights, "the Panel of Experts should seek information from the ILO, including any pertinent available interpretative guidance, findings or decisions adopted by the ILO".[100] This is a self-conscious effort to promote greater legal certainty in the field. It is also recognized in the North American Free Trade Agreement of 2008 that in the dialogue procedure the parties may request the ILO for independent verification of compliance.[101] Proliferation of labour standards does not necessarily lead to normative fragmentation and institutional confrontation.[102] International actors are generally cautious to not overrule one another's standards too lightly.

Thirdly, the existing supervisory mechanism of the ILO, which evaluates the performance of member states under ratified ILO conventions, could also provide a useful reference as to the observance of ILO standards by states under other commitments. The Committee of Experts on the Application of Conventions and Recommendations may also "serve as a source of guidance" when it comes to the interpretation of labour provisions.[103] It is acknowledged in FTAs that trade partners "may establish cooperative arrangements with the ILO and other competent international or regional organisations to draw on their expertise and resources".[104]

Proliferation of labour standards has brought many challenges to the door of the ILO. The ILO should endeavour to reinstate itself as a central institution for economic and social theories as well as for labour standards. Its intellectual capability is as essential as its normative mandate. It is important for the ILO to perform a legal-diplomatic role in promoting convergence of normative understandings about labour, economy and society among different institutions. In doing so, stressing the social dimension of globalization would, one may hope, lead to the revitalization of not only the ILO but workers at large in the economic and political life of the world.

[100] EU-Canada Comprehensive Economic and Trade Agreement, 30 October 2016.

[101] North American Free Trade Agreement, 30 November 2018.

[102] For example, in the US-Guatemala labour arbitration, the arbitration panel expressly refers to the ILO 1998 Declaration to ascertain the meaning of right to strike. See Arbitral Panel established pursuant to Chapter 20 of the CAFTA-DR (2017).

[103] Agustí-Panareda et al. (2014).

[104] See for example, EU-Canada Comprehensive Economic and Trade Agreement, 30 October 2016.

References

ADB (2003) Social protection strategy 2001. Available at: https://www.adb.org/sites/default/files/institutional-document/32100/social-protection.pdf. Accessed 6 May 2018

AFL–CIO (1998) Executive Council statement on Asian financial crisis (29 January 1998). Available at: https://aflcio.org/about/leadership/statements/asian-financial-crisis. Accessed 6 May 2020

AFL–CIO (2000) Executive Council statement on equitable, democratic, sustainable development (18 February 2000). Available at: https://aflcio.org/about/leadership/statements/equitable-democratic-sustainable-development. Accessed 6 May 2020

African Development Bank Group (2013) Integrated safeguards system: policy statement and operational safeguards. Available at: https://www.afdb.org/fileadmin/uploads/afdb/Documents/Policy-Documents/December_2013_-_AfDB%E2%80%99S_Integrated_Safeguards_System__-_Policy_Statement_and_Operational_Safeguards.pdf. Accessed 6 May 2020

Agustí-Panareda J, Ebert FC, LeClercq D (2014) Labour provisions in free trade agreements: fostering their consistency with the ILO standards system. International Labour Office, Geneva

AIIB (2016) Environmental and social framework (February 2016). Available at: https://www.aiib.org/en/policies-strategies/_download/environment-framework/20160226043633542.pdf. Accessed 6 May 2020

Alston P (2004) Core labour standards and the transformation of the international labour rights regime. Eur J Int Law 15(3):457–522

Arbitral Panel established pursuant to Chapter 20 of the CAFTA-DR (2017) Final report of the Panel in the matter of Guatemala – issues relating to the obligations under Article 16.2.1(a) of the CAFTA-DR (14 June 2017). Available at: https://legacy.trade.gov/industry/tas/Guatemala%20%20%E2%80%93%20Obligations%20Under%20Article%2016-2-1(a)%20of%20the%20CAFTA-DR%20%20June%2014%202017.pdf. Accessed 6 May 2020

Blackett A, Trebilcock A (eds) (2015) Research handbook on transnational labour law. Edward Elgar, Cheltenham

Bolle MJ (2016) Overview of labor enforcement issues in free trade agreements. Available at: https://fas.org/sgp/crs/misc/RS22823.pdf. Accessed 6 May 2020

Breining-Kaufmann C (2007) Globalisation and labour rights: the conflict between core labour rights and international economic law. Hart, Oxford

BSTDB (2014) Environmental and social policy (1 January 2014). Available at: https://www.bstdb.org/Environmental_Policy_Feb2016.pdf. Accessed 6 May 2020

Chen Y (2018) The making of global public authorities: the role of IFIs in setting international labor standards. In: Quayle P, Gao X (eds) AIIB yearbook of international law vol 1: good governance and modern international financial institutions. Brill Nijhoff, Leiden

Compa L (1995) Going multilateral: the evolution of U.S. hemispheric labor rights policy under GSP and NAFTA. Conn J Int Law 10(2):337–364

Craig JDR, Lynk SM (eds) (2006) Globalization and the future of labour law. Cambridge University Press, Cambridge

Davis KE, Kingsbury B, Merry SE (2012) Indicators as a technology of global governance. Law & Soc Rev 46(1):71–104

de Wet E (2010) Governance through promotion and persuasion: the 1998 ILO declaration on fundamental principles and rights at work. In: von Bogdandy A, Wolfrum R, von Bernstorff J, Dann P, Goldmann M (eds) The exercise of public authority by international institutions. Springer, Heidelberg

Ebert FC (2015) International financial institutions' approaches to labour law: the case of the International Monetary Fund. In: Blackett A, Trebilcock A (eds) Research handbook on transnational labour law. Edward Elgar, Cheltenham

Ebert FC (2018) Labour standards and the World Bank. Analysing the potential of safeguard policies for protecting workers. In: Gött H (ed) Labour standards in international economic law. Springer, Cham

EBRD (2003) Environmental policy 2003. Available at: http://www.ebrd.com/downloads/research/policies/policy.pdf. Accessed 6 May 2020
EBRD (2006) Sustainability report 2006. Available at: https://www.ebrd.com/publications/annual-report-2006.pdf. Accessed 6 May 2020
EBRD (2008a) Sustainability report 2008. Available at: https://www.ebrd.com/downloads/research/sustain/sr08e.pdf. Accessed 6 May 2020
EBRD (2008b) Environmental and social policy (12 November 2008). Available at: http://ebrd.com/downloads/research/policies/2008policy.pdf. Accessed 6 May 2020
EIB (2013) Environmental and social handbook. Available at: http://www.eib.org/attachments/strategies environmental_and_social_practices_handbook_en.pdf. Accessed 6 May 2020
Fahlbeck R, Mulder BJ (2009) Labour and employment law in Sweden. Juristförlaget, Lund
GATT (1987) Relationship of internationally-recognized worker rights to international trade: communication from the United States, L/6196 (3 July 1987)
Hepple B (2005) Labour laws and global trade. Hart, Oxford
IFC (2006) Performance standards on social & environmental sustainability (30 April 2006). Available at: https://www.ifc.org/wps/wcm/connect/3f3419f4-6043-4984-a42a-36f3cfaf38fd/IFC%2BPerformance%2BStandards.pdf?MOD=AJPERES&CVID=jkC.Eka&id=1322803957411. Accessed 6 May 2020
IFC (2012) Performance standards on environmental and social sustainability (1 January 2012). Available at: https://www.ifc.org/wps/wcm/connect/c02c2e86-e6cd-4b55-95a2-b3395d204279/IFC_Performance_Standards.pdf?MOD=AJPERES&CVID=kTjHBzk. Accessed 6 May 2020
ILO (n.d.-a) Ratifications of C087 – Freedom of Association and Protection of the Right to Organise Convention, 1948 (No. 87). Availabe at: http://ilo.org/dyn/normlex/en/f?p=NORMLEXPUB:11300:0::NO:11300:P11300_INSTRUMENT_ID:312232:NO. Accessed 6 May 2020
ILO (n.d.-b) Ratifications of C098 – Right to Organise and Collective Bargaining Convention, 1949 (No. 98). Available at: http://ilo.org/dyn/normlex/en/f?p=NORMLEXPUB:11300:0::NO:11300:P11300_INSTRUMENT_ID:312243:NO. Accessed 6 May 2020
ILO (1994) Defending values, promoting change: social justice in a global economy: An ILO agenda: Report of the Director-General. International Labour Office, Geneva
ILO (1997) ILO, standard setting and globalization: Report of the Director-General, International Labour Conference, 85th Session, Geneva, 1997
ILO (1998) Report of the Committee on the Declaration of Principles, International Labour Conference, Record of Proceedings, 86th Session, Geneva, 1998
ILO (2008) Freedom of association in practice: lessons learned, global report under the follow-up to the ILO Declaration on Fundamental Principles and Rights at Work. International Labour Office, Geneva
ILO (2016) Statement on the World Bank environmental and social policy (8 August 2016). Available at: http://www.ilo.org/global/about-the-ilo/newsroom/statements-and-speeches/WCMS_508328/lang%2D%2Den/index.htm. Accessed 6 May 2020
ILO (2017) Handbook on assessment of labour provisions in trade and investment arrangements. International Labour Office, Geneva
IMF (2017) The IMF and social protection: 2017 evaluation report. Available at: https://ieo.imf.org/en/our-work/Evaluations/Completed/2017-0724-the-imf-and-social-protection. Accessed 6 May 2020
International Labour Office (2007) Fourth item on the agenda – the United Nations and reform: developments in the multilateral system, World Bank Doing Business report: the employing workers indicator (GB.300/4/1), Governing Body, 300th Session, Geneva, November 2007
ITUC/Global Unions (2007) The IFIs' use of Doing Business to eliminate workers' protection: analysis of Doing Business 2008 and new country evidence. Available at: https://www.ituc-csi.org/IMG/pdf/doing_business.pdf. Accessed 6 May 2020
ITUC/Global Unions (2014) Major weaknesses in World Bank's draft labour standards safeguard (22 July 2014). Available at: https://consultations.worldbank.org/sites/default/files/consulta-

tion-template/review-and-update-world-bank-safeguard-policies/submissions/ess2-wb_ituc-critique_0714.pdf. Accessed 6 May 2020

Kryvoi Y (2009) The World Bank and the ILO: two visions of employment regulation. In: Blanpain R, Grant C (eds) Fixed-term employment contracts: a comparative study. Vanden Broele, Bruges

La Hovary C (2018) The ILO's mandate and capacity: creating, proliferating and supervising labour standards for a globalized economy. In: Gött H (ed) Labour standards in international economic law. Springer, Cham

Maupain F (2005) Revitalization not retreat: the real potential of the 1998 ILO declaration for the universal protection of workers' rights. Eur J Int Law 16(3): 439–465.

Maupain F (2013) The future of the international labour organization in the global economy. Hart, Oxford

Murphy H (2014) The World Bank and core labour standards: between flexibility and regulation. Rev Int Polit Econ 21(2):399–431

NDB (2016) Environmental and social framework (11 March 2016). Available at: https://www.ndb.int/wp-content/themes/ndb/pdf/ndb-environment-social-framework-20160330.pdf. Accessed 6 May 2020

NIB (2012) Sustainability policies and guidelines (21 March 2012). Available at: https://www.nib.int/filebank/56-Sustainability_Policy_Guidelines-2012.pdf. Accessed 6 May 2020

OECD (1996) Trade, employment, and labour standards: a study of core workers' rights and international trade. OECD Publications Service, Paris

Santos A (2019) The lessons of TPP and the future of labor chapters in trade agreements. In: Kingsbury B, Malone D, Mertenskötter P, Stewart RB, Streinz T, Sunami A (eds) Megaregulation contested: global economic ordering after TPP. Oxford University Press, Oxford

Standing G (2008) The ILO: an agency for globalization? Development and Change 39(3):355–384

Swepston L (1994) The future of ILO standards. Monthly Labour Rev 117(9):16–23

Tapiola K (2018) The teeth of the ILO – the impact of the 1998 ILO Declaration on Fundamentals Principles and Rights at Work. International Labour Office, Geneva

Tham JC, Ewing KD (2020) Labour provisions in trade agreements: neoliberal regulation at work? Int Org Law Rev 17(1):153–177

UN (1995) Report of the World Summit for social development, Copenhagen, 1995

United States Senate (1957) Contribution to the international labour organization: hearings before the committee on foreign relation. United States Government Printing Office, Washington

United States Senate (1995) Reorganization and revitalization of America's Foreign Affairs Institutions: hearings and markups before the committee on foreign relations and the subcommittee on international operations of the committee on foreign relations. United States Government Printing Office, Washington

Ushakova T (2018) The Trans-Pacific partnership labour chapter: a new paradigm of the social clause? In: Gil y Gil JL (ed) Trade and labour standards: new trends and challenges. Cambridge Scholars Publishing, Newcastle upon Tyne

Wade R (1997) Greening the Bank: the struggle over the environment, 1970–1995. In: Kapur D, Lewis JP, Webb R (eds) The World Bank: its first half century, vol 2: perspectives. Brookings Institution Press, Washington

World Bank (2003) Doing business in 2004: understanding regulation. Available at: https://www.doingbusiness.org/content/dam/doingBusiness/media/Annual-Reports/English/DB04-FullReport.pdf. Accessed 6 May 2020

World Bank (2009) Doing business 2010: reforming through difficult times. Available at: https://www.doingbusiness.org/content/dam/doingBusiness/media/Annual-Reports/English/DB10-FullReport.pdf. Accessed 6 May 2020

World Bank (2010) Doing business 2011: making a difference for entrepreneurs. Available at: https://www.doingbusiness.org/content/dam/doingBusiness/media/Annual-Reports/English/DB11-FullReport.pdf. Accessed 6 May 2020.

World Bank (2013) World Bank's safeguard policies review and update – expert focus group on the emerging area labor and occupational health and safety (23 March 2013). Available at: https://

consultations.worldbank.org/sites/default/files/meetings/Safeguards_Focus_Group_Labor_Indonesia_Summary_Final.pdf. Accessed 6 May 2020
World Bank (2014a) World Bank's safeguard policies review and update, proposed environmental and social framework: Background paper (2 September 2014)
World Bank (2014b) Review and update of the world bank's environmental and social safeguard policies, Phase 2 – Feedback summary: consultation with government officials from Belgium and the Netherlands (10 November 2014). Available at: https://consultations.worldbank.org/sites/default/files/consultation-template/review-and-update-world-bank-safeguard-policies/en/meetings/safeguard_review_phase_2_consultations_2014_-_feedback_summary_brussels_government_and_multilaterals_meeting_november_10.pdf. Accessed 6 May 2020
World Bank (2014c) Environmental and social framework: setting standards for sustainable development – First draft for consultation (30 July 2014). Available at: http://documents.worldbank.org/curated/en/311951468331802393/pdf/898130BR0CODE200Box385287B00PUBLIC0.pdf. Accessed 6 May 2020
World Bank (2015a) World Bank's safeguard policies review and update – labour expert group (21 January 2015). Available at: https://consultations.worldbank.org/sites/default/files/consultation-template/review-and-update-world-bank-safeguard-policies/en/meetings/safeguards_london_focus_group_meeting_jan_21.pdf. Accessed 6 May 2020
World Bank (2015b) Meeting of labour experts on the second draft of the World Bank's environmental and social standard 2: labour and working conditions (ESS 2) (18 September 2015). Available at: https://consultations.worldbank.org/sites/default/files/consultation-template/review-and-update-world-bank-safeguard-policies/en/meetings/ess2_meeting_report_0915.pdf. Accessed 6 May 2020
World Bank (2015c) United States comments on World Bank Safeguards review – Phase 2 (26 March 2015). Available at: https://consultations.worldbank.org/sites/default/files/consultation-template/review-and-update-world-bank-safeguard-policies/submissions/2015-3-26_usg_comments_on_draft_wb_esf_final.pdf. Accessed 6 May 2020
World Bank (2015d) Review and update of the World Bank's environmental and social safeguard policies, Phase 3, Feedback summary: Consultation with Chinese governmental officials (27 October 2015). Available at: https://consultations.worldbank.org/sites/default/files/consultation-template/review-and-update-world-bank-safeguard-policies/en/meetings/final_feedback_summary_for_phase_3_consultation_with_chinese_central_government_and_institutions_in_beijing_october_27.pdf. Accessed 6 May 2020
World Bank (2015e) Review and update of the World Bank's safeguard policies environmental and social framework: Environmental and social framework (Proposed second draft), Summary of phase 2 Consultations and Bank management responses (31 July 2014–1 March 2015)
World Bank (2015f) Safeguard policies' review consultations: Nordic Baltic position as of February 23, 2015. Available at: https://consultations.worldbank.org/sites/default/files/consultation-template/review-and-update-world-bank-safeguard-policies/submissions/nordic_baltic_comments_of_27_feb_2015.pdf. Accessed 6 May 2020
World Bank (2015g) Review and update of the World Bank's environmental and social safeguard policies, Phase 3, Feedback summary: consultation with Chinese provincial governments and implementing agencies (29 October 2015). Available at: https://consultations.worldbank.org/sites/default/files/consultation-template/review-and-update-world-bank-safeguard-policies/en/meetings/final_feedback_summary_for_phase_3_consultation_with_chinese_provincial_governments_and_pmos_in_yunnan_october_29.pdf. Accessed 6 May 2020
World Bank (2016a) Comments/observations of the Government of Bangladesh on the World Bank's environmental and social safeguard framework and other related documents (6 January 2016). Available at: https://consultations.worldbank.org/sites/default/files/consultation-template/review-and-update-world-bank-safeguard-policies/submissions/comments_from_govt_of_bangladesh_on_essf-01_12_15.pdf. Accessed 6 May 2020
World Bank (2016b) Review and update of the World Bank's safeguard policies environmental and social framework: Environmental and social framework (Proposed third draft), Summary

of phase 3 Consultations and Bank management responses (4 August 2015–15 March 2016). Available at: http://documents.worldbank.org/curated/en/748451469107442841/pdf/107175-BR-R2016-0145-IDA-R2016-0198-Box396279B-PUBLIC.pdf. Accessed 6 May 2020

Yifeng Chen is an Associate Professor at the Peking University Law School. Before joining Peking University, He was a post-doctoral researcher at the University of Helsinki from 2010–2013 and continues to serve as a docent in international law at the University of Helsinki. He worked as a senior research fellow on the Academy of Finland research project "Implementation of ILO core labour standards in China: legal architecture and cultural logic" (2012–2015). He has worked extensively on history of labour and social laws in Republican China and ILO core labour rights. His fields of interest include history and theory of international law, international organizations, international and comparative labour law.

An Accidental Revolution: The ILO and the Opening Up of International Law

Jan Klabbers

Contents

1 Introduction

Contrary to popular opinion, the role of law, both in domestic societies and in international affairs, is not first and foremost about constraining action. Law is not about telling people how to behave, and inflicting punishment when they behave differently—not solely, at any rate. To think this, as many do, is to view criminal law as the template for law generally. Instead, much of the law, both in domestic societies and in international affairs, follows a different template, and is about facilitating action.

What is more, in addition to (or in the process of) facilitating action, law also helps to structure the way we think about things. We cannot begin to think of the state without invoking the criteria for statehood; we cannot seriously discuss agreement without bearing legal concepts of treaty or contract in mind; and we cannot characterize the military presence of state A in state B without some term from the legal vocabulary, and it matters a great deal which exact term we employ, for calling something an "invasion" or an "attack" evokes different associations than labelling the same act an "intervention".[1] That is not to say our conversations should stop at

[1] Klabbers (2015a), pp. 488–506.

J. Klabbers (✉)
University of Helsinki, Helsinki, Finland
e-mail: jan.klabbers@helsinki.fi

T. Halonen, U. Liukkunen (eds.), *International Labour Organization and Global Social Governance*, https://doi.org/10.1007/978-3-030-55400-2_6

those legal concepts, for sometimes doing so might lapse into awkwardness or worse, as when a court proves unable to think of genocide in terms other than those of the 1948 Genocide Convention and thus suggests that an earlier genocide was probably not "really" a "genocide".[2] That said, though, rules, norms and decisions[3] set the tone for any social conversation. Rules, norms and decisions also tend to have distributive effects. Any authoritative decision will allocate something of value, whether financial or social. A decision by a country club to admit someone as a member will change that individual's relative standing in the community, and a decision by the UN Educational, Scientific and Cultural Organization (UNESCO) to admit Palestine as a member adds legitimacy to Palestine's position in global politics. A decision by a pizza parlour to change its opening hours or update its menu will convenience some and inconvenience others. Enacting a rule that inaugurs driving on the right side of the road will disadvantage some car manufacturers, even if one might hold that the rule is a textbook example of a coordination rule. And a decision by the World Health Organization (WHO) to declare a pandemic will come to affect the producers of vaccines, may send shockwaves through the tourism industry, and may even inaugurate a full-blown economic crisis, as the 2020 Covid-19 crisis vividly illustrates.[4]

Given that rules, norms and decisions invariably have distributive effects, they are typically employed as weapons and arms in struggles for power and hegemony between people (states, companies, organizations, individuals) with diverging political agendas. Those weapons may have long fuses, and their effects may only manifest themselves over time, but this makes them only more effective, for the most effective form of power is the power to influence how people think about things.[5] No lesser authority than John Maynard Keynes was well aware of this, explicitly dedicating his analysis of the Versailles settlement to influencing the minds of future generations of policy makers.[6]

With this in mind, the creation of the ILO can be seen as a crucial step in the development of public international law, and its singular relevance resides in having sensitized international law to addressing the situation of individuals, whether as employers or as workers. The relevance of the ILO is not just that it helped create and enforce labour rights, although it did and does that too. But part of its relevance also resides in something else, on a deeper level so to speak; this has little to do with labour rights per se, but rather more with opening up international law, with making visible that international law is not just about inter-state relations. The ILO is probably the first international organization—the first manifestation of international

[2] See European Court of Human Rights (somewhat softened by the Grand Chamber), *Perinçek v. Switzerland* (App. No. 27510/08), Judgment, 15 October 2015; for discussion, see Klabbers (2017a).

[3] This refers to the classic study by Kratochwil (1989). See also Kratochwil (2018).

[4] Klabbers (2020).

[5] Lukes (1974).

[6] Keynes (1920), p. 279: "[...] the true voice of the new generation has not yet spoken, and silent opinion is not yet formed. To the formation of the general opinion of the future I dedicate this book."

law—to take individuals and companies seriously, thus paving the way for the involvement of international law in more recent years with individuals, something we now almost take for granted. Human rights involve the individual, as do international criminal law, EU law, the law on investment protection, et cetera. It is impossible to prove (and silly even to try) that none of this would have happened without the ILO. But what can be demonstrated is that the ILO marked a significant step in the creation of the individual as an entity of relevance to international law.[7]

In what follows, I will substantiate that particular claim, demonstrating first that the international legal vocabulary prior to the ILO's creation did not facilitate thinking about individual rights under international law, in thrall as it was to the idea that international law only operated between states and would only affect states, in their capacity as states. Thereafter, I will discuss the creation of the ILO, indicating just how creating the ILO marked a seismic shift. This is followed by a discussion as to how and why the international legal vocabulary—the landscape—changed with the establishment of the ILO.

2 Dualism and Its Discontents

Traditionally, international law was always nominally concerned with relations between states. International law, in a collated textbook definition from the late nineteenth century, was the law made by states, to regulate relations between states, and for the benefit of those states. Oppenheim, e.g., in the second edition of his classic treatise published in 1912, defined international law as "the body of customary and convention rules which are considered legally binding by civilized States in their intercourse with each other".[8] And he adds that international offices are created to give effect to treaties establishing unions between states.[9] There was not a hint of a suggestion here that international law, or the work of those international offices, might come to affect others than states. States enjoyed, one might say, considerable epistemic priority. Other actors never even entered the picture in any serious manner, except as religious or historical exceptions.[10] After all, so the logic went, only states can go to war. Only states can conclude treaties. Only states can proclaim territorial waters.

[7] I will studiously refrain from using the term 'subject' of international law, as this often merely functions as a placeholder.

[8] Oppenheim (1912), p. 3. Oppenheim's influence can hardly be over-estimated: see García-Salmones Rovira (2013).

[9] Oppenheim (1912), p. 516.

[10] Think of the Holy See or the Maltese Knights. Intriguingly, upon its creation the League of Nations was categorized in the same manner in one of the great historical overviews of international law. See Verzijl (1969).

The epistemic priority of the state also extended to international organizations. These were always derivative creatures, deriving their existence and powers from the states that founded them.[11] What is more, international organizations were not supposed to have any outward-radiating effect. If the early international organizations were not endowed with international legal personality, it was because no one considered such personality necessary, for the good reason that organizations were not supposed to interact directly with anyone other than their member states—not with third states, not with other international organizations, and not with the citizens of their member states either. And for much the same reason, they had no treaty-making powers to speak of. Each organization was supposed to be a universe onto itself (*res inter alios acta*), with the only relationships envisaged being those between the organization and its member states, but never with the outside world.[12] This still applied, in 1945, to the UN, set up as an entity of universal scope both substantively and in terms of geographical reach, but with few treaty-making powers or even provisions recognizing that there existed a world outside the organization (military agreements were envisaged to regulate troop contributions, and some coordination with other organizations was planned, but not much more) and no explicit grant of international legal personality. The latter only came about after the intervention of the International Court of Justice, in 1949.[13]

And when international law even deigned to think about individuals, it was only in relation to the state, only as state representatives. This applied formally with respect to protection of diplomats or the conclusion of treaties. It applied more artificially with the protection of property abroad: injuring the individual was seen as injuring the state, and entitling the state (though not the individual) to take action.[14] Not everyone was convinced. Philip Jessup could write in the late 1940s that if injury to the state was the true basis of responsibility for injury to aliens, then "the measure of damages to be paid for an injury would vary with the importance of the role played by the injured individual in the life of the state of which he is a citizen."[15]

All this suggested that international law and domestic law would never need to be in touch with one another: international law stayed on the inter-state level, and the rest was the concern of domestic law.[16] The logic of thinking of international and domestic law as separate systems made some sense, on the surface level—otherwise it could not have survived for very long. It did however rest on one condition: it only

[11] Klabbers (2015b).

[12] Klabbers (2016), pp. 618–634.

[13] International Court of Justice, *Reparation for Injuries Suffered in the Service of the United Nations*, Advisory Opinion, 11 April 1949. In International Court of Justice Reports of Judgments, Advisory Opinions and Orders 1949. See also Klabbers (2017b), pp. 105–121.

[14] Permanent Court of International Justice, *Case of the Mavrommatis Palestine Concessions*, Judgment, 30 August 1924. In Publications of the Permanent Court of International Justice, Series A, No. 2.

[15] Jessup (1948), p. 9.

[16] And when the UK started to pioneer the prosecution of slave traders, it did so largely on the basis of its domestic law, even if to some extent bilateral treaties proved supportive. See Martinez (2014).

made sense as long as no one asked why states would go to war and who would be affected by war; or why states concluded treaties or proclaim territorial waters, and who would be affected. Once those questions are asked, the idea of there being purely inter-state activities which form the natural realm of international law, quickly turns into a conceit.

But founded on the logic that international affairs are by definition merely inter-state affairs,[17] no situation could possibly bring the individual into contact with international law, as indeed Triepel observed and further theorized in 1899.[18] The universes of domestic law and international law were considered to be hermetically sealed off. Empirically, Triepel noted, domestic law deals with relations involving individuals, and international law is limited to regulating relations between states. On the rare occasions that a treaty would aim to do something for individuals, it would have to be transformed into domestic law. This idea came to be known as dualism, and is still maintained (albeit often in somewhat softened form) in many states. The gist is that domestic legal orders can only work on the basis of instruments recognized as legally valid within those domestic orders, typically Acts of Parliament, Governmental Decrees, and the like. As a result, other instruments, regardless of their provenance (but typically referring to international legal instruments) must be transformed into acts recognized as legally valid by and within the legal order concerned; a treaty must be transformed into an Act of Parliament or Governmental Decree in order to be recognized as valid within that legal order, and in order to create rights or obligations for individuals within that legal order.

This was never a fully accurate or convincing picture, but it worked until the 1920s, and generated an understandable popularity. It entailed that domestic parliaments, which had fought hard and long to acquire a say over domestic legislation, could not be outflanked or overruled by governments entering into international commitments. Over international commitments, after all, typically those same parliaments had no influence. If dualism thus respected concerns about local democracy (at least nominally), a side-effect was the re-affirmation of the role of the state and a re-affirmation of the strict separation between international and domestic law.

Triepel himself pointed out that his theory was empirically-based; it was built on the finding that there actually were no contacts between the international and the domestic legal order. These things are always in the eye of the beholder (in that few matters in law really have an empirical correspondent independently from the particular theory in which empirical observations play a role, and tend to be much more dependent on hermeneutics[19]), but Triepel made a forceful case. He did note, however, that the minorities treaties concluded in connection with the re-drawing of Europe's map at Versailles could come to affect individuals.[20] But, he wrote in 1923, that moment had not yet arrived. International law still dealt only with states.

[17] Note how, as so often in legal thought, the conclusion is already inherent in the premises.

[18] Triepel (1899).

[19] Klabbers (forthcoming).

[20] Triepel (1923), pp. 73–121.

Naturally, this strict separation between the domestic and international spheres also affected the creation of international organization, including the very early river commissions addressing issues of navigation, safety, and security. The idea behind the river commissions was to establish common rules for navigation, and this was done by ordering the states to legislate—thus keeping the separate spheres intact. The Final Act of the Congress of Vienna 1815, e.g., proves illustrative. Article 108 provides that states set up common regimes for navigation, while Article 110 made clear that "uniformity" was key. On the Rhine, the Neckar, and other rivers, the exact same rules should apply with respect to all states concerned, both relating to navigation and in terms of policing. Article 111 further underlined the need for harmonization: "Les droit sur la navigation seront fixé d'une maniére uniforme, invariable, et [...] indépendente de la qualité différente des marchandises [...]".

Note the way Article 111 was written: what was needed here was for the river commissions to set standards, and then for the riparian states to turn these into law—no one had given any thought to allowing river commission to set those standards directly. Instead, the instruction of Article 111 was directed at states: states would have to set in uniform manner the navigation rights.

This pattern continued throughout the nineteenth and early twentieth century. The International Telegraphic Union (ITU), the Universal Postal Union (UPU), International Bureau of Weights and Measures, the Union of International Transport by Rail, the International Sugar Union, the International Institute for Agriculture: all late-nineteenth century and early twentieth century creations were thought of as creations of states, affecting those very states (the member states) in their very capacity as states. And in the case where they were not thought of in state-centric terms, as creatures of states, then they were not considered part of international law. The Red Cross (created in 1863 by Henri Dunant and Gustave Moynier[21]) is a prime example; another is the Institut de Droit International, set up in Ghent in 1873.[22]

Still, every now and then a minor crack became visible. The US, e.g., was reluctant to join the ITU,[23] mostly because the telegraph networks in the US were in private hands, while in other member states they were usually under public control. This seemed to signify, however dimly, a realization that the work of the ITU might affect network operators. It was also said of the Union of International Transport by Rail that its dispute settlement procedures made no distinction between governmental and nongovernmental railway administration, again suggesting a dim realization that the Union's work may affect entities within the state, and not just those states themselves.[24]

Indeed, the strict separation between the international and domestic spheres was never very realistic. It seems fairly obvious that the setting of postal rates by UPU not only affects Denmark and Japan and Nigeria, but also affects individuals and

---

[21] Bennett (2005).

[22] The latter is memorably depicted in Koskenniemi (2001).

[23] It eventually joined in 1908.

[24] Jessup (1956), p. 17.

businesses as senders of letters and packages, and it seems fairly obvious that prices set by the sugar union affect the market price for sugar and therewith immediately affect consumers and producers.[25] But while there was inevitably an indirect effect on individuals, it was always mediated by the state—and indeed, international law did not have any other mechanisms at its disposal. Edwin Borchard, writing in 1940, summarized the dualist position, noting that "dualists will admit that many of the rules of treaty and international law are devised for and accrue to the benefit of individuals, they nevertheless insist that only States may become spokesmen for these rules and advantages."[26]

The thought that international law could have direct effect on individuals was, so to speak, not yet thought, and would only first be thought by the Permanent Court of International Justice (PCIJ) in the late 1920s.[27] And even then, the PCIJ, when developing its position on direct effect, did so with considerable ambivalence: whether or not a provision of a treaty would be directly effective would depend on the intentions of the drafters of that provision, and those drafters were, invariably, states. This was, in other words, not quite the empirical position Triepel had in mind. Or rather, more accurately perhaps, the empirical evidence could be manipulated by states: a provision where international and domestic law would be in contact could still be said not to be directly effective if there would be an indication that parties wished to preclude direct effect.[28]

3 Establishing the ILO

But in 1919, when the ILO was created in Versailles, this was still something for the future.

Versailles saw the creation of the League of Nations, the clearly still highly state-centric creature to guarantee collective security.[29] But Versailles also saw the creation of the ILO. But why the ILO, and why not an international organization for, say, global health? Or for maritime affairs or arms control? Why even create a second organization, in addition to the League, and why not simply a convention to treat workers decently? In other words, what was the problem to which this international organization, the ILO, was expected to be the solution?

The obvious answer—or the beginning of an answer—is that the ILO marks a response to the October revolution of 1917, and reading contemporary papers and

---

[25] See also the illuminating study by Fakhri (2014).

[26] Borchard (1940), p. 139.

[27] Permanent Court of International Justice, *Jurisdiction of the Courts of Danzig*, Advisory Opinion, 3 March 1928. In Publications of the Permanent Court of International Justice, Series B, No. 15.

[28] And this in turn has been put to effective use by some states in the form of so-called "non-self-executing declarations". See further Klabbers (2017c), pp. 325–326.

[29] Note however that the League too could not avoid addressing the plight of individuals, in particular those living under the Mandate system. For a fine historical analysis, see Pedersen (2015).

books, there is a clear sense of urgency on this point. Part of the idea behind the ILO was to set it up as an answer to the red threat, to communism. As David Morse, long-time Director-General of the ILO, much later put it in admirably bureaucratic and anodyne style, "there was general recognition that the ferment and instability which characterized the world of labor and industry in 1918 and 1919, particularly in Europe, called for immediate and constructive action."[30] The idea was to make the working man happy, or rather, to make sure he would not be so unhappy that he would turn to communism. In practice, this entailed decent working conditions: it is surely no coincidence that the first ILO conventions deal with working hours, unemployment, maternity protection, and night work. The first recommendations addressed similar matters and tried to protect against dangerous materials, aiming to protect works working with anthrax, lead, white phosphorus.[31]

But still, a set of intellectual problems emerged. The drafters realized all too well that economic circumstances differ from country to country, from state to state. Thus, there is a quasi-natural competitive obstacle that needs to be overcome. What made things more difficult still was the realization that protecting labour comes at the expense of capital, and that the costs and benefits might not be evenly distributed. Some industries would be harder hit than others; for some industries, protecting workers would come at bigger costs than for other industries, not because those others would have been doing so earlier, but because they would be less dependent on night work, or would be less involved with dangerous materials. A third problem that emerged revolved around colonialism: some of the bigger states benefitted from cheap labour being available in their colonies. In fact, as one of the founding fathers, Britain's George Barnes, openly confessed in relation to the imperial issue: "To be quite candid, our motives were not altogether humanitarian."[32]

Instead, while the communist threat was perceived as very real, it had to be met in such a way as not to distort global competition. The same George Barnes notes, in his work on the ILO written a few years after its creation, that the "need had arisen for levelling out industrial competition between the nations by raising the conditions of labour in the lower-paid countries",[33] and diagnosed the problem as being related to mass manufacturing by "cheap Eastern labour".[34]

This proved quite a riddle. Capitalism requires competition, after all, and one of the more obvious arenas for industrial competition is in the sphere of labour, both by keeping wages low and not spending much on decent working conditions. Yet allowing for the race to the bottom to occur was thought to play in the hands of

---

[30] Morse (1969), p. 4. Contrast this with another view: "The spectre of Bolshevism was a powerful stimulus for being responsive to the requests of labor." Jacobson (1984), p. 302.

[31] Note that some of these (night work, phosphorus) had already been the subject of conventions concluded during the early 1900s under auspices of the International Association for Labour Legislation.

[32] Barnes (1926), p. 45.

[33] Ibid., p. 37.

[34] Ibid., p. 45. By Eastern, he meant Asian.

communism, putting the capitalist world economy at risk. It seemed a veritable catch-22: either allow for unhampered competition and invite communism to take over, or limit competition as far as labour issues are concerned and in that way implicitly accommodate communism as well. Clearly, this left a delicate balancing act: infusing just enough worker protection into the system so as to save the system: too much would make the capitalist economy collapse, and too little would have pretty much the same result. The logic was well-put by a contemporary observer, Leonard Woolf: "If it is in the interest of every State to regulate the conditions of employment within its territory, but it is prevented from doing so unless all the other States do likewise", so Woolf wrote, "then clearly the solution ought to be found in unification of the Labour laws of the different countries through international agreements."[35]

One possible way—hypothetically at any rate—to solve the problem was to leave it entirely to the market, and open the borders for unmitigated migration. If the capitalist logic would work, after all, then people would move to the place where there would be work and a decent wage. This, however, was never realistic. As John Hobson observed at the time, Asia may be a "rich reservoir" of labour, but "the difficulty of procuring the general assent of civilized nations to "an open door" for Asiatic labour would, of course, be insuperable"[36]; Hobson's casual use of the term "of course" spoke volumes.

One thing that became reasonably clear was that a single convention on worker's rights was unlikely to do the trick. What was needed instead was a careful and continued balancing of the interests of workers, capital and states, and this, in turned, required permanent management, not a one-off arrangement in the form of a treaty; for a single treaty could never be comprehensive enough to cover all industries, cover all kinds of situations that might arise, and accommodate all conflicting interests.[37] And the balancing act turned out to be quite successful. As historian Emily Rosenberg concludes, generally speaking "the organization supported a liberal capitalist system operating through cooperating national states [...] and opposed an alternative transnational labor movement that was being promoted through the Soviet Union's Third International."[38]

The ILO's success in performing the balancing act of navigating between unfettered labour competition possibly leading to communism, and adopting communism *tout court*, it can be said with considerable hindsight, was due to the combination of organizational form and tripartite structure—even if the precise limits of this organizational form remained subject to debate, and resulted in the

[35] Woolf (1916), p. 183.

[36] Hobson (1915), p. 143.

[37] Klabbers (2019a), pp. 629–646.

[38] Rosenberg (2012), p. 35. Mazower agrees, noting that the ILO followed "a precarious corporatist course between hostile capitalists to its right and revolutionary socialists to its left". Mazower (2012), p. 152.

Permanent Court of International Justice being asked several questions.[39] Paul Reinsch, arguably the most influential thinker about international organizations law,[40] had already a decade earlier drawn attention to the difficulties involved in making labour legislation on an ad hoc basis, one treaty at the time.[41] Hence, the organizational form was pivotal, for only a permanent organization facilitates permanent management. Only a permanent organization could manage and massage the constantly changing configurations of interests involving capital, labour and government.[42]

This dovetailed nicely with a second invention: tripartism. During World War I, the major industrialized states had all seen fit to mobilize labour and capital for the war effort, and in Britain in particular this was welcomed as an experiment well worth repeating. Britain made an effort to transplant the model to the nascent ILO, also because it realized that if it were alone among the major powers to continue to practice tripartism, it might suffer a competitive problem. Cox puts it well: "As the leading trading nation, Britain might have been disadvantaged in world markets if a peacetime prolongation of tripartism were to have the effect of raising labor costs. Hence the concern of British officials to internationalize the experiment."[43]

One unexpected implication of the establishment of tripartism is that it cemented a place for non-state interests in the work of an international organization. It became clear that the interests of all stakeholders could not be reduced to those of the member states. This had been the traditional idea: what is good for the state, is good for everyone within the state, and things can be kept on the inter-state level. But with the ILO now, it was clearly understood that whatever the ILO would decide, adopt and promulgate, would affect workers and capital—not just the state and its competitive position. Thus, tripartism set in motion an accidental revolution, by incorporating other than direct state interests in the institutional structure of an

[39] Permanent Court of International Justice, *Competence of the ILO in regard to International Regulation of the Conditions of Labour of Persons Employed in Agriculture*, Advisory Opinion, 12 August 1922. In Publications of the Permanent Court of International Justice, Series B, No. 2; Permanent Court of International Justice, *Competence of the ILO to Examine Proposal for the Organization and Development of the Methods of Agricultural Development*, Advisory Opinion, 12 August 1922. In Publications of the Permanent Court of International Justice, Series B, No. 3. It also took a few years for the Court itself to come to terms with the institutional element: it only started to develop a theory of powers in Permanent Court of International Justice, *Competence of the ILO to Regulate Incidentally the Personal Work of the Employer*, Advisory Opinion, 23 July 1926. In Publications of the Permanent Court of International Justice, Series B, No. 13.

[40] On the relevance of Reinsch, see Klabbers (2014a).

[41] Reinsch had noted that the International Association of Labor Legislation was "admirably fitted" for harmonizing and unifying labour legislation, probably precisely because of its permanence—although he shied away from drawing the conclusion explicitly. Reinsch (1911), p. 47.

[42] Maupain hints at much the same when discussing the difficulties inherent in making international labour legislation, resulting either in free riding (and thus disturbing competitive balances) or in the adoption of the lowest common denominator. As a result, what was needed was a constitutional structure that allowed for persuasion while leaving sovereign prerogatives intact. See Maupain (2013), p. 15.

[43] Cox (1987), p. 75.

international organization, and therewith acknowledging that the work of this organization did not just affect member states in their mutual relations, but could potentially affect every worker in every member state, and every employer in every member state.

The revolution was *accidental* in that the inspiration behind tripartism had been to secure Britain's competitive position, rather than any grand design about popular consultation or great philosophy of the *quod omnes tangit* variety.[44] It owed little to good intentions or to visionary inspiration. And it was a *revolution* because it opened the door to changing conceptions of international law. The establishment of the ILO slowly created the possibility for thinking of international law as directly affecting the real lives, the real interests, the real blood and real guts, of real people. If until the creation of the ILO international law could still with some sense be said to apply to inter-state relations only (if only because everyone seemed to agree that this was the case), once the ILO was created this was no longer possible: the toothpaste had been squeezed out of the tube; and once the bell tolls, its sound can no longer be unheard.

4 The Changing Landscape

It is generally acknowledged that the ILO's tripartite structure was, at the time, unique—and by and large it still is, at least in the sense in which the formal constitution of an international organization formally involves representatives of social actors other than government representatives, as the ILO does with insisting that states representations include representatives from government, labour and capital.[45]

But if the ILO's structure is still unique, the past century has developed several variations on the same theme. In some organizations, it is possible for states to be represented by specialists: meteorologists in the case of the World Meteorological Organization; police officers in the case of Interpol (which actually started as cooperation between police forces[46]), and in the WHO there is an understanding that states strive to be represented by people with a medical background. More generally, the Universal Postal Union was the brainchild of the US Postmaster General in the 1860s, Mr. Montgomery Blair,[47] while most of the

[44] This is the sort of trope (*quod omnes tangit ab omnibus approbatur*; "what touches all should be approved by all") that might come to play a role in different settings. One well-known manifestion is the slogan "no taxation without representation".

[45] This, in turn, may give rise to domestic struggles about who gets to represent labour and capital; those struggles sometimes reach international tribunals, and have done so right from the start: Permanent Court of International Justice, *Designation of the Workers' Delegate for the Netherlands at the Third Session of the International Labour Conference*, Advisory Opinion, 23 July 1926. In Publications of the Permanent Court of International Justice, Series B, No. 1.

[46] Martha (2010).

[47] Sly (1927), pp. 395–436.

directors-general of the International Telecommunications Union (ITU) established in 1865, have been engineers or physicists.[48] More generally, moreover, many organizations have specialized organs where the expectation is that members have a specialist background, as with the Radio Regulations Board in ITU or the various emergency committees advising the director-general of the WHO in accordance with the 2005 International Health Regulations.[49]

In other organizations, different mechanisms are opted for. Thus, the ITU allows for corporate membership of a kind, set up much like customer loyalty schemes with several tiers; an estimated 700 companies and academic institutions thus form part of the broader ITU circle; in addition to membership by states, in this way social interests (or, by and large more accurately, corporate interests) are directly represented. The European Forest Institute has two categories of membership: state membership, and membership of research institutions (it started out as an association of research institutes), requiring an intricate institutional balance when it comes to decision-making. Some organizations participate in joint ventures with private sector actors: these are particularly prevalent in the global health domain, where an important role is played by the Bill and Melinda Gates Foundation.[50] More generally, organizations often participate in particular projects with a range of partners from both the public and the private sectors. One prominent example is that of the Contact Group on Piracy off the Somali Coast, a somewhat loose network comprising a number of intergovernmental organizations but also comprising seafarers' unions and, naturally perhaps, Lloyd's of London, the leading maritime insurance company. Some organizations, moreoever, are quite dependent on financial contributions from agents other than their member states: UNHCR's annual budget derives for some 10% from private donations, while an organization such as the International Organization for Migration (IOM) has to be largely self-sufficient, and can only do so by positioning itself as a private actor and collaborating with private actors.[51]

And then there are organizations where societal interests are represented in all sorts of advisory organs or through consultative status: think of the EU's Committee of the Regions, or the hundreds of actors having consultative status with the UN General Assembly or the UN Economic and Social Council. Member states might be happy to include domestic actors in their national missions, whether senators or parliamentarians from the opposition or more straightforward interest representatives. And where consequential decisions are taken, lobbying is never far away. This applies not only to private interests, but also to civil society actors: it is a public secret that the Assembly of States Parties to the International Criminal Court[52] is in thrall to the many NGOs dedicated to bringing

[48] Klabbers (unpublished paper, 2019, on file with the author).

[49] On the latter, see Klabbers (2019b).

[50] Andonova (2017).

[51] Klabbers (2019c).

[52] Note that for these purposes there is no problem in treating the ICC and its ASP as an international organization. For other purposes doing so might be less easily justifiable: to the extent that

an end to impunity, and getting various crimes and classes of victims to be recognized as relevant.

The ILO was pioneering in its tripartite structure, ensuring the representation of social interests in its standard-setting work. But it was also pioneering in a different sense: it was the first organization explicitly devoted to improving the plight of individuals, regardless of the then prevailing template according to which international organizations would only affect member state interests. At any rate, that was always an impossible conceit: it may be the case that the telegraphic pipelines regulated by the ITU were mostly publicly owned, but the senders and recipients of telegraph messages were, most often, private individuals and private companies.[53] At the end of the day, the impact of the ITU was not just on its member states (although it was that too), but also on the citizen, the industrialist, the reporter.[54] Likewise, the work of the UPU could not but affect those who send and receive postcards, letters and parcels from abroad—the state plays an intermediary role as a conduit for all those private interests, but it would be difficult to maintain the fiction that a missing postcard or a lost parcel would come to hurt the national interest. This was, admittedly, the prevailing mindset, but was always more ideological than real. Indeed, even the navigation rules of the early river commissions affected shipping far more than national states, and more often than not, that was the very motive behind their creation. Sayre unapologetically wrote, a century ago and at the eve of the creation of both the League of Nations and the ILO, that the various international river commissions operating in China were set up to protect western commercial interests—and these did not even bother to include China among their member states.[55]

In a sense then, by focusing on protection of workers, the ILO made explicit what was already implicit with other organizations: that the ultimate addressee and stakeholder would be the individual, whether as worker or as industrialist, with member states mostly involved as conduit. The member states make the rules together and have to implement them in one way or another, but it would be insufficient to say that the regime only affected those member states, and not any one residing within them. With the ILO this was, no doubt, the result of turning vice into virtue: the focus on the individual was occasioned by the distrust of other states. The risk of facilitating "free riding" was simply too big to organize worker protection in any other way than through the combination of continuous law-making while

organizations exercised delegated powers and act under instructions from their member states, one might be reluctant to include judicial institutions.

[53] In his pathbreaking study, Murphy demonstrates just how strongly the ITU has been the pivot around which the first global telecommunications revolution revolved in the late nineteenth century, effectively establishing the global legal infrastructure for the entire business. See Murphy (1994).

[54] It is hardly a coincidence that around the same time, international journalism came off the ground, and Reuter's started to become a household name. See, e.g., Wilson (2016).

[55] Sayre (1919).

respecting sovereignty, and to do so through a permanent entity rather through a single convention or small group of related conventions.

It was only once the ILO had sensitized international law to the possibility of piercing through the mystifying veil of the state, that the international community could come to think of protecting human rights. And even then it took a while still, with direct protection of individual human rights hesitantly[56] emerging in the late 1940s and early 1950s and, importantly, after another World War had underlined that perhaps concerted action would be required to prevent further atrocities, and states could not be relied on to do so themselves.[57] The Universal Declaration, the European Convention on Human Rights, the Genocide Convention and the Refugee Convention, they were all concluded within a period of 3 years or so (1948–1951), and all have protection of the individual as their common topic. Importantly though, they all envisage a conduit role for the state, and to the extent that international monitoring was put in place, it would be considerably later, and typically on a voluntary basis, through additional optional protocols. The point for present purposes though is that these instruments were only possible once the ILO had opened the windows and let in a fresh breeze, diluting the stale air of a strong inter-state conception of international law.

This would be further developed by the EU, that wonderful and occasionally somewhat tragic experiment in governance and authority beyond the state.[58] The original treaties, concluded in the 1950s, already manifested that public and private participation were envisaged, for instance in the form of the revolutionary creation of the European Parliament. But the EU went considerably further, as its Court of Justice (itself open to other than inter-state complaints) acknowledged in a string of classic cases, including *Van Gend & Loos* and *Costa* v *ENEL*, both decided early in the EU's existence.[59] The existence of a preliminary reference procedure, allowing domestic courts to consult the CJEU, was pivotal, as was the positing of the direct effect of EU law in the domestic legal orders of the member states. The legal instruments envisaged would create Union-wide legislation (or at least harmonize the domestic laws of the member states), and the Commission would have enforcement powers across national boundaries. The EU truly marked an astonishing experiment, but it is important to note that, as with most other experiments, it stands on the shoulders of predecessors: the EU would have looked different, and possibly less adventurous, without the earlier pioneering work that went into creating the ILO.

[56] Some suggest it was not until the 1970s that human rights seriously became successful. See Moyn (2010).

[57] The interbellum minorities treaties were always exceptional: the ambition was not so to protect individuals, but to counterbalance the viccisitudes of great power politics at Versailles.

[58] Klabbers (2019d), pp. 25–41.

[59] European Court of Justice, *NV Algemene Transport- en Expeditie Onderneming van Gend & Loos v. Netherlands Inland Revenue Administration* (Case 26/62), Judgment, 5 February 1963; European Court of Justice, *Flaminio Costa* v *E.N.E.L* (Case 6-64), Judgment, 15 July 1964.

This is so not only because its main *auctor intellectualis*, Jean Monnet, worked for a while close by the ILO as the Deputy Decretary-General of the League of Nations, and may have had a look at how the ILO was set up and how it worked in practice.[60] It is also not only because the EU was created with considerable Christian-democrat input, and had an ideological affinity for social cooperation between stakeholders in accordance with Christian doctrine.[61] This may have been given an extreme form earlier by Mussolini, turning corporatism into fascism, but the basic corporatist idea so central to Christian political philosophy characterizes both the ILO and the EU—albeit probably for different reasons.[62]

But the main reason why the EU would have looked differently without the ILO experience is the circumstance highlighted above: the ILO was the first to clear the state-centric cobwebs from international organization, and the first to open up international law to recognition and embrace of interests other than those presumed to be of states. One might argue, of course, that states have few interests of their own, other than the circular concept of the *raison d'état*. That is an insight that is slowly gaining acceptance, but credit where credit is due: possibly the first venue where this was made visible was the ILO, partly because it incorporated social interests through its tripartite structure, and partly because it may well have been the first venue (forced by circumstances, but nonetheless…) which recognized that individuals could be addressed under international law. While there is some ground to suggest that the bilateral treaties of the nineteenth century aided in bringing slavery to an end, these treaties were still the result of paternalist impulses. What made the ILO different was that to the extent that paternalist thought was involved, it was counterbalanced by the self-interests of employers. The ILO took the form, eventually, of states making law to protect individuals, but beneath this surface layer, the ILO's output is the outcome of serious social struggle between labour and capital—governance beyond the state, rather than governance between states.

5 To Conclude

It may well be the case that, as far as the concrete standard-setting and effectiveness thereof is concerned, the ILO may have become somewhat marginalized over the course of its first century.[63] There are some topics related to labour where one wishes

---

[60] Monnet's biographer does not discuss the ILO, but does cite Monnet's confession that while at the League, he "did not understand the politics of Versailles, only the economics". Duchêne (1994), p. 364.

[61] While not stressing the Christian-democrat element, an excellent discussion of the ordo-liberalism that went into the EU and later the WTO is Slobodian (2018).

[62] See Cox (1987), p. 101. Above I explain that tripartism (the ILO's version) owes much to British interests; that logic cannot apply to the EU, which saw the light without much British participation.

[63] Klabbers (2014b), pp. 181–196.

it would have been a little more active, a little more vocal—the link between labor and migration comes to mind, which can scarcely be left to individual governments alone or to the International Organization for Migration, with its mandate to ensure orderly migration but with less of a humanitarian impulse governing its activities. Likewise, the ILO may still be adapting to transformations of the global political economy, with global supply chains and the emergence of the platform economy changing the scene.[64]

But even so, the world would look differently, and most likely considerably worse, without the ILO. Its main contribution has not just been in concrete standard-setting, but perhaps even more so, as this paper has argued, in opening up the closed universe of inter-state international law, therewith paving the way for later developments,[65] including refugee protection, human rights protection, and the emergence of the EU. And that is, by any standard, quite an achievement.

References

Andonova LB (2017) Governance entrepreneurs: international organizations and the rise of global public-private partnerships. Cambridge University Press, Cambridge

Barnes GN (1926) History of the international labour office. Williams and Norgate, London

Bennett A (2005) The Geneva Convention: the hidden origins of the Red Cross. Sutton Publishing, Stroud

Berliner D, Greenleaf AR, Lake M, Levi M, Noveck J (2015) Labor standards in international supply chains: aligning rights and incentives. Edward Elgar, Cheltenham

Borchard E (1940) The relation between international law and municipal law. Va Law Rev 27(2):137–148

Cox RW (1987) Production, power, and world order: social forces in the making of history. Columbia University Press, New York

Duchêne F (1994) Jean Monnet: the first statesman of interdependence. Norton, New York

Fakhri M (2014) Sugar and the making of international trade law. Cambridge University Press, Cambridge

García-Salmones Rovira M (2013) The project of positivism in international law. Oxford University Press, Oxford

Hobson JA (1915) Towards international government. George Allen & Unwin, London

Jacobson HK (1984) Networks of interdependence: international organizations and the global political system, 2nd edn. Knopf, New York

Jessup PC (1948) A modern law of nations. Macmillan, New York

Jessup PC (1956) Transnational law. Yale University Press, New Haven

Keynes JM (1920) The economic consequences of the peace. Macmillan, London

Klabbers J (2014a) The emergence of functionalism in international institutional law: colonial inspirations. Eur J Int Law 25(3):645–676

Klabbers J (2014b) Marginalized international organizations: three hypotheses concerning the ILO. In: Liukkunen U, Yifeng C (eds) China and ILO fundamental principles and rights at work. Bulletin of Comparative Labour Relations, No. 86. Kluwer Law International, Alphen aan den Rijn

[64] See Berliner et al. (2015) and Srnicek (2016).

[65] A different question is what sort of individual is sponsored and supported by international law: see Urueña (2012).

Klabbers J (2015a) Intervention, armed intervention, armed attack, threat to peace, act of aggression, and threat or use of force: what's the difference? In: Weller M (ed) Oxford handbook of the use of force in international law. Oxford University Press, Oxford
Klabbers J (2015b) The EJIL foreword: the transformation of international organizations law. Eur J Int Law 26(1):9–82
Klabbers J (2016) Theorising international organisations. In: Orford A, Hoffmann F (eds) The Oxford handbook of the theory of international law. Oxford University Press, Oxford
Klabbers J (2017a) Doing justice: bureaucracy, the rule of law and virtue ethics. Rivista di Filosofia del Diritto 6(1):27–50
Klabbers J (2017b) Transforming institutions: autonomous international organisations in institutional theory. Cambridge J Int Comp Law 6(2):105–121
Klabbers J (2017c) International law, 2nd edn. Cambridge University Press, Cambridge
Klabbers J (2019a) International organizations and the problem of privity: towards a supra-functionalist approach. In: Politakis GP, Kohiyama T, Lieby T (eds) ILO 100 – law for social justice. International Labour Office, Geneva
Klabbers J (2019b) The normative gap in international organizations law: the case of the WHO. Int Org Law Rev 16(2):272–298
Klabbers J (2019c) Notes on the ideology of international organizations law: the International Organization for Migration, state-making, and the market for migration. Leiden J Int Law 32(3):383–400
Klabbers J (2019d) The European Union in the law of international organizations: misfit or model? In: Wessel RA, Odermatt J (eds) Research handbook on the European Union and international organizations. Edward Elgar, Cheltenham
Klabbers J (2020) The second most difficult job in the world: reflections on COVID-19 (2020). Int Humanit Leg Stud:1–12
Klabbers J (forthcoming) Constitutionalism as theory. In: Dunoff JL, Pollack MA (eds) International legal theory: foundations and frontiers. Cambridge University Press, Cambridge
Klabbers J (unpublished paper, 2019, on file with the author) International Organizations, Epistemic Structures
Koskenniemi M (2001) The gentle civilizer of nations: the rise and fall of international law 1870–1960. Cambridge University Press, Cambridge
Kratochwil FV (1989) Rules, norms, and decisions: on the conditions of practical and legal reasoning in international relations and domestic affairs. Cambridge University Press, Cambridge
Kratochwil FV (2018) Praxis: on acting and knowing. Cambridge University Press, Cambridge
Lukes S (1974) Power: a radical view. Macmillan, London
Martha RSJ (2010) The legal foundations of Interpol. Hart, Oxford
Martinez JS (2014) The slave trade and the origins of international human rights law. Oxford University Press, Oxford
Maupain F (2013) The future of the international labour organization in the global economy. Hart, Oxford
Mazower M (2012) Governing the world: the history of an idea. Allen Lane, London
Morse DA (1969) The origin and evolution of the I.L.O. and its role in the world community. Cornell University – New York State School of Industrial and Labor Relations, Ithaca
Moyn S (2010) The last utopia: human rights in history. Harvard University Press, Cambridge
Murphy CN (1994) International organization and industrial revolution: global governance since 1850. Polity, Cambridge
Oppenheim L (1912) International law: a treatise, 2nd edn. Longmans, Green, London
Pedersen S (2015) The guardians: the League of Nations and the crisis of empire. Oxford University Press, Oxford
Reinsch PS (1911) Public international unions, their work and organization: a study in international administrative law. Ginn and Company, Boston
Rosenberg ES (2012) Transnational currents in a shrinking world: 1870–1945. Harvard University Press, Cambridge

Sayre FB (1919) Experiments in international administration. Harper & Brothers, New York
Slobodian Q (2018) Globalists: the end of empire and the birth of neoliberalism. Harvard University Press, Cambridge
Sly JF (1927) The genesis of the Universal Postal Union: a study in the beginnings of international organization. In: International Reconciliation 233. Carnegie Endowment for International Peace, New York
Srnicek N (2016) Platform capitalism. Polity, Cambridge
Triepel H (1899) Völkerrecht und Landesrecht. C.L. Hirschfeld, Leipzig
Triepel H (1923) Les rapports entre le droit interne et le droit international. In: Recueil des Cours, vol 1. Brill Nijhof, Leiden
Urueña R (2012) No citizens here: global subjects and participation in international law. Martinus Nijhoff, Leiden
Verzijl JHW (1969) International law in historical perspective. Subjects of international law, vol 2. Brill Nijhoff, Leiden
Wilson B (2016) Heyday: the 1850s and the dawn of the global age. Basic Books, New York
Woolf L (1916) International government. George Allen & Unwin, London

Jan Klabbers is Professor of International Law at the University of Helsinki, and a leading scholar in the field of law of international organizations. He was Deputy Director of the Erik Castrén Institute of International Law and Human Rights. From 2006 to 2011, he was Director of the Academy of Finland's Centre of Excellence in Global Governance Research. He has also acted as the Academy of Finland Martti Ahtisaari Professor at the University of Helsinki, working on a project on global virtue ethics. Professor Klabbers is the author of several books and articles on the law of international organizations, and is currently engaged in a large-scale project investigating how relations between international organizations and the private sector come to affect legal practice and the theory underlying the law of international organizations.

Postscript

Joseph E. Stiglitz

Contents

The Covid-19 epidemic has exposed many of the deficiencies in national and global economic and social systems. For all its wealth, the seemingly richest and most powerful country, the United States, became the global leader in infection rates, deaths, and an increased unemployment rate. The riots that broke out across the country in May, 2020, signified a country greatly divided. Money can buy a lot of things, but evidently it alone can't buy health or social harmony.

The reasons for the dismal failure of the US are manifold: Unfettered capitalism led to unbridled inequalities and unmatched instabilities, exemplified by the 2008 financial crisis in which ordinary citizens who lost their homes and jobs bore the brunt of the costs; corporations and banks have been allowed to exploit their customers, their workers, and the planet that we share;[1] but among the most important reasons for the US failures is the inadequacy of its systems of social protection and the denigration of the rights of workers.

The connections are, unfortunately, all too clear.[2] The US is the only advanced country that doesn't recognize the right to health care as a basic human right. And while President Obama tried to extend access to health care for all, President Trump and his party have worked hard to reduce it, so that 3 years after taking office, some

[1] I expand on many of the themes raised in this post script in my recent book, Stiglitz (paperback edition, with new introduction, 2020).

[2] For a further discussion of these issues, see Stiglitz (2020).

J. E. Stiglitz (✉)
Columbia University, New York, NY, USA
e-mail: jes322@columbia.edu

T. Halonen, U. Liukkunen (eds.), *International Labour Organization and Global Social Governance*, https://doi.org/10.1007/978-3-030-55400-2_7

two million more Americans are without health insurance. The minimum wage in the United States is lower than it was 60 years ago, adjusted for inflation, and that means working fulltime doesn't generate a livable income. Large fractions of Americans live paycheck to paycheck. On top of that, America is one of the few advanced countries not to mandate paid sick leave. The combination—living paycheck to paycheck and no paid sick leave—is lethal, because it means that employees infected with Covid-19 go to work when they possibly can. They have to, if they are going to feed their families and pay their bills.

Congress recognized the problem, and passed a law requiring paid sick leave, but just for workers sick with Covid-19. Then, under pressure from America's biggest and richest companies, they exempted employers with more than 500 employees—precisely the employers who could most easily pay for it. Thus, almost half of all workers were exempted. This story tells a lot about the short-sightedness and the selfishness of capitalism American-style—even the corporations lost. For instance, when meat packing companies, which failed to provide masks and protective gear for their workers, became hot spots of the disease, the plants had to shut down. This cost the companies far more than they would have saved by not providing paid sick leave. With such pervasive myopia, it explains why government must play a role.

The corporate decisions might have been different if workers had had a say on company boards. The workers might have been able to explain that not providing health insurance or paid sick leave was penny wise but pound foolish, because a healthy labor force is a more productive labor force. Governance matters. Who makes the decisions affects what decisions are made. And good economic governance has to pay attention to social consequences.

Indeed, the objective of our economic system should not be to just increase GDP—or corporate profits. A well-functioning economic engine should be designed to raise the living standards—broadly understood—of all citizens. GDP, it is now recognized, is a poor measure of societal well-being, or even economic performance more narrowly defined.[3]

It used to be that workers' perspectives could be presented strongly by unions. Here in New York City, the butchers' union made it clear during the pandemic that their workers weren't going to work unless employers provided masks. But in the US and many other countries, unions have been weakened to the point where they are unable to adequately advocate on behalf of workers.

1 Globalization

Underlying the problems that Covid-19 has exposed so dramatically is the weakening of the power of workers—their bargaining power vis-a-vis corporations in the marketplace, and their political power, as corporate money has held increasing sway in America's money-driven politics. (I should emphasize: I write about America

[3] See Stiglitz et al. (2010, 2018).

both because it is the country I know best, but also because it has become the paradigm for what happens with unbridled capitalism. Too many countries, especially before the 2008 crisis, looked to the US as a model, to their detriment. Those countries that have most closely emulated the American model have the highest levels of inequality and the worst performance across a wide range of social dimensions.[4])

There are, in turn, multiple intertwined reasons for this weakening of workers' political and economic power. The weakening of unions has had political consequences; imbalances in wealth and economic power inevitably translate into imbalances of political power, and the consequence is legislation that makes workers' collective action more difficult—more difficult to unionize and to achieve gains at the bargaining table.

Poorly managed globalization is one of the important reasons for the change in the power of workers. As emerging markets and less developed countries became more integrated into the global economy, workers in advanced countries were pitted against workers from the developing world. Standard theory predicted that this would lower wages of workers in the advanced countries, especially if they were unskilled. Indeed, this process would continue until wages (adjusted for skills) were the same everywhere—that's the ideal of a well-functioning market. Of course, the advocates of unfettered globalization never "advertised" that this would be the outcome. Rather, they told another story, of globalization making countries richer, of benefits trickling down to everyone in society. There was never any theory or evidence behind these arguments, they were just shiny lures—and now four decades have shown to be true what serious economists had predicted all along: stagnant incomes for large fractions of workers and a hollowing out of the middle class.[5]

Of course, globalization could have been managed in other ways, but it was managed by and for corporate interests. These interests, for instance, succeeded in getting stronger property rights protections outside the United States than corporations had within the US. The companies could then threaten to move abroad unless their workers gave concessions on wages and working conditions.

Again, the pandemic has illustrated the short-sightedness of this unbalanced globalization, where the United States was incapable of quickly producing the masks, the protective gear, the ventilators, and the tests that the country required. A focus on short-term profits had made the economy far less resilient, far less able to respond.

2 Global Cooperation

Meanwhile, the pandemic has illustrated both the negative and positive sides of global cooperation. The pandemic and its economic consequences will not be contained until it is contained everywhere, and unless there is a global economic

[4] Overall, countries with greater inequality also have poorer economic performance, more narrowly defined. See, e.g., Stiglitz (2012).

[5] For a more extensive discussion of the points raised in this paragraph, see Stiglitz (2017).

recovery. Pandemics and global environmental issues, like climate change, are arenas where global cooperation is absolutely essential. Fortunately, the world has, over the past hundred years, created international organizations to manage global cooperation. In this arena the lead organization is the World Health Organization, but the multilateral financial institutions have played an important role in providing finance for poor countries to strengthen their health care systems.

At the same time, scientists around the world are cooperating in the attempt to quickly discover a vaccine, develop better tests, and find therapies that are effective against the disease.

That's the positive side. On the negative side, the American president pulled out of WHO, and has undertaken policies to ensure that the US has first access to any vaccine—rather than that the vaccine goes to where it is most critical, e.g. to health care workers. While other countries have committed themselves to a Covid-19 patent pool—to ensure that the knowledge will be available to all, with appropriate licensing fees—so that the scourge will be eliminated as quickly as possible, the US has focused on strengthening intellectual property claims.

Almost 20 years ago, I served on the World Commission on the Social Dimensions of Globalization established by the ILO. This 101-year-old organization is distinctive in bringing together governments, workers, and businesses to address the common problems we face, and working to achieve solutions that are in the common interest. Earlier discussions of globalization had largely forgotten its social dimensions. As I pointed out earlier, unfettered globalization—or more accurately, globalization managed for the benefits of large corporations—can result in a race to the bottom, with wages and working condition deteriorating for many in the advanced countries. The environment, too, will be a victim of this kind of globalization. We didn't fully see that even the economy can be a victim, as became apparent during the global financial crisis a short five years after the issuance of our report.

One area in which we had a healthy discussion was intellectual property, where the particular concern was access to medicines, precisely the issue raised by the patent pool. It should be clear that most of the key advances in this area rest on foundations of publicly funded research. Moreover, there are better ways to conduct testing, at lower costs, and with fewer conflicts of interest, than by allowing the very companies that stand to profit from a drug to be responsible for its testing. The drug companies do perform a role in bringing the drugs to market, though the way they do this often results in exorbitant prices and actually impedes innovation.

Our Commission concluded that the intellectual property regime established as part of the Uruguay Round that had created the WTO, the so-called Trade Related Intellectual Property system (TRIPS), was badly flawed. We needed "TRIPS-minus," that is, a system of intellectual property rights that also guaranteed the rights of access, especially for life-saving drugs. The drug companies, not surprisingly, supported by the US and some other governments, have, to the contrary, succeeded in creating in the subsequent years a "TRIPS-plus" regime, one that further restricts access to medicines, a regime that may prove particularly costly in this pandemic.

3 Concluding Comments

Crises provide moments for reflection. The 2020 pandemic is a major crisis—a health crisis precipitating a major economic and social crisis. It is a global phenomenon, requiring a global response. It is a crisis that highlights the inequalities in our society. The virus is not an equal opportunity infector—it goes after people in poor health; and in societies like the US, marked by high levels of health and income inequalities, there are many in poor health.

Had there been more global cooperation before the pandemic—cooperation in which *all* voices were heard, not just the corporations'—we might have built a world marked by less inequality. We might have constructed more resilient economies that were better able to cope with the pandemic and with its economic consequences.

Now, the imperative is to construct a post-pandemic world marked by more global cooperation, with better social governance, with the voices of all stakeholders being heard. The ILO provides a model of what can be done.

References

Stiglitz JE (2012) The price of inequality: how today's divided society endangers our future. W. W. Norton & Company, New York

Stiglitz JE (2017) Globalization and its discontents revisited: anti-globalization in the era of trump. W. W. Norton & Company, New York

Stiglitz JE (2020) Four priorities for pandemic relief efforts. Working Paper April 2020. Roosevelt Institute, New York. Available at: https://rooseveltinstitute.org/wp-content/uploads/2020/04/RI_Four-Priorities-for-Pandemic-Relief-Effort-WP-202004.pdf. Accessed 4 June 2020

Stiglitz JE (paperback edition, with new introduction, 2020) People, power, and profits: progressive capitalism for an age of discontent. W. W. Norton & Company, New York

Stiglitz JE, Fitoussi JP, Sen A (2010) Mismeasuring our lives: why GDP doesn't add up. Report of the Commission of the Measurement of Economic Performance and Social Progress. The New Press, New York

Stiglitz JE, Fitoussi JP, Durand M (2018) Beyond GDP: measuring what counts for economic and social performance. OECD Publishing, Paris

Joseph E. Stiglitz was the 2001 Nobel Laureate in Economics. He was Chairman of the Council of Economic Advisers from 1995 to 1997, and Chief Economist and Senior Vice-President of the World Bank from 1997 to 2000. In 2008, he chaired the Commission on the Measurement of Economic Performance and Social Progress. In 2009, he was appointed by the President of the UN General Assembly as chair of the Commission of Experts on Reform of the International Financial and Monetary System. Stiglitz is now Co-Chair of the High-Level Expert Group on the Measurement of Economic Performance and Social Progress, OECD. He is a Professor at Columbia University and is Chief Economist of the Roosevelt Institute.

The manufacturer's authorised representative in the EU is Springer Nature Customer Service Centre GmbH, Europaplatz 3, 69115 Heidelberg, Germany. If you have any concerns regarding our products, please contact ProductSafety@springernature.com

Printed and bound by CPI Group (UK) Ltd, Croydon, CR0 4YY
30/09/2026
02225466-0020